South
Toward
Home

Also by Julia Reed

But Mama Always Put Vodka in Her Sangria!

Ham Biscuits, Hostess Gowns, and
Other Southern Specialties

South
Toward
Home

*Adventures and
Misadventures in
My Native Land*

Julia Reed

St. Martin's Press
New York

www.stmartins.com

Designed by Mary A. Wirth

LIBRARY OF CONGRESS CATALOGING-IN-PUBLICATION DATA

Names: Reed, Julia, author.
Title: South toward home : adventures and misadventures in my native land / Julia Reed.
Description: First edition. | New York : St. Martin's Press, 2018. | Includes bibliographical references.
Identifiers: LCCN 2017060165| ISBN 9781250166340 (hardcover) | ISBN 9781250166364 (ebook)
Subjects: LCSH: Reed, Julia—Homes and haunts—Southern States. | Reed, Julia—Travel—Southern States. | Southern States—Description and travel. | Southern States—Civilization. | Southern States—Social life and customs. | Southern States—Humor.
Classification: LCC F209.5 .R45 2018 | DDC 975—dc23
LC record available at https://lccn.loc.gov/2017060165

Our books may be purchased in bulk for promotional, educational, or business use. Please contact your local bookseller or the Macmillan Corporate and Premium Sales Department at 1-800-221-7945, extension 5442, or by email at MacmillanSpecialMarkets@macmillan.com.

First Edition: July 2018

10 9 8 7 6 5 4 3 2 1

For my father, Clarke Reed,
the Silver-Haired Daddy of the Delta

Contents

· ·

Part Three. Southern Sustenance

Part Four. The South in All Its Glory—Or Not

Part Five. Fun

Acknowledgments

· ·

Sid Evans was my first editor at *Garden & Gun*. He not only hatched the idea of the columns collected in this book, he also kept the magazine afloat—and on the map—during the toughest of times.

David DiBenedetto, Sid's successor as the magazine's editor-in-chief, is the best friend, sounding board, drinking buddy, confidante, and collaborator a girl could hope to have. The magazine—and its writers—have thrived under his leadership.

Rebecca Darwin guides the ship with a steady hand and passionate heart.

This is my fourth outing with my intrepid book editor Michael Flamini. His unfailing enthusiasm, patience, talent, and trust have been true gifts. He is also an unrivaled dining companion and invaluable menu consultant!

Jon Meacham has been both my actual and my shadow editor

for almost two decades. I will never be able to thank him enough for his clarity, his advice (though he claims I never take it), and for his steadfast friendship. Keith Meacham is herself an excellent editor and true blue friend—and provider of luxurious safe harbor whenever I am in Nashville.

My agent Binky Urban keeps the trains, and me, on track. It is no small feat but she pulls it off it with her usual grace and good humor.

Too many people to name either appear on these pages or have inspired them. I am lucky indeed to be surrounded by so much love, support, and good humor, and so many stalwart hearts.

Finally, I remain forever grateful that my father landed in the Mississippi Delta, the place I so happily call home, and that he convinced my mother to make a life with him there. They are two of the most extraordinary people I'll ever know.

Foreword

· ·

Tell me a story.
In this century, and moment, of mania,
Tell me a story.
Make it a story of great distances, and starlight. . .
Tell me a story of deep delight.

—ROBERT PENN WARREN

The poet, novelist, and critic Robert Penn Warren wrote those lines in 1969, and they were published in a volume of his entitled *Audubon*. I am, it is true, a sucker for Warren—*All the King's Men*, the epic 1946 novel about Willie Stark, a Huey Long-like figure who seeks to do his best, albeit imperfectly, in a fallen world, remains perhaps the seminal book of my life—but I can honestly say that I have never encountered a finer description of the duty of the writer than the verse above: to tell stories of great distances, of starlight, and, finally, of deep delight, however tragic and ultimately incomplete life may be on this side of Paradise.

The book you are reading now is in the Warren tradition of deep delight. With her distinctive voice, her sense of humor

and of humanity, and her persistent—if largely unacknowl-
edged, for that would give away the game—good cheer about
the world's great and small joys, Julia Reed has emerged as one
of the country's most astute and insightful chroniclers of the
things that matter most. Whether the topic is what we eat, how
we live, or why we believe, Julia has, in her books and in her
wildly popular column in *Garden & Gun*, pulled off what
her fellow Mississippian William Faulkner set out to do when
he said that he wanted to take a "postage stamp of native soil,"
of his fictional Yoknapatawpha County, as a particular stage
on which to dramatize great human themes.

Julia's postage stamp, though, is even larger than Faulkner's.
To switch metaphors, her canvas is the whole of the South,
stretching from the dives of New Orleans up through her
beloved Delta and winding up, naturally, in the northern
reaches of Virginia, at the Madeira School for girls. Who else
but Julia could be a trusted guide through such a sprawling mass
of America, never putting a Manolo Blahnik-shod foot wrong
in limning the triumphs and absurdities of culture? I can't think
of a single soul.

Whether her subject is Scotch whiskey, the opossum, or the
mad politics, mournful music, and out-of-the-way cafés and
bars of the South, Julia unerringly finds the universal in the
particular. In a way, she's a foreign correspondent in her own
land, filing dispatches about the sacred and the profane—and
revealing, often subtly, the porous border between the two.
The mark of a great journalist is the capacity to see what should
be evident to everyone but somehow isn't—not until a keener
eye and a sharper sensibility casts fresh light on what lies be-

fore us in plain sight, suddenly giving readers the fabled flash of recognition.

That's Julia's formidable gift—the gift, as Shelby Foote once put it in a letter to Walker Percy describing the writer's craft, of teaching others how to see. Because of her, our vision is clearer, our senses heightened, our lives charmed and enchanted. And what more, in the end—or even in the beginning or in the middle—could we ask of a writer than that?

Nothing. Nothing more. For decades I have been struck by how many people come up to me to bear unsought witness to Julia's power—the readers of her work who, on learning that I am fortunate enough to be her friend, want to tell me how important, how wonderful, how *indispensable* they find her voice. That irreplaceable, unmatched voice is the one you will hear in the following pages. Alternately funny and wise, charming and knowing, transporting and illuminating, Julia has, in this collection, given us yet another great gift. It is a gift, you will soon come to see, of deep delight.

As is, inescapably, Julia herself.

—*Jon Meacham*

Introduction

. . . .

In 1967 Willie Morris wrote a memoir, *North Toward Home,* in which he recalled his childhood in the Mississippi Delta, a place with its share of dark history, but also one of abiding grace and goodness, humor and eccentricity. Like Willie, I grew up in the Delta, in Greenville, about seventy miles up the road from his birthplace in Yazoo City and, like Willie, I went north, first to Washington, D.C., and then to Manhattan, not toward home exactly, but for a career in journalism and what I hoped would be a rich, full life. It was. But a few years after Willie returned home, I came back South too, first to New Orleans, where I have lived off and (mostly) on since the early 1990s and, more recently, to my beloved Delta, where I'm building a house.

Until I came back, I don't think I realized how much I'd missed the landscape and the sense of community, the humor and the good-heartedness, the agricultural scent of earth and chemicals more powerful to me than any of Proust's madeleines.

Most of all, I'd missed the fact that fun was so damn easy to get up to. I had some fun with Willie a time or two before he left us in 1999, but his prose is what I remember best. I frequently quote his line that "it's the juxtapositions that get you" down here, because they sure as hell still abound.

A couple of years ago, for example, I found myself slap in the middle of some typically jarring contradictions when my good buddies Roy Blount, Jr. and William Dunlap and I served on a panel together in Jackson, Mississippi, the city Willie ultimately called home. Our assigned topic was fairly loose, but we knew we'd be touching on possums—Roy and I have both written about them (there's an essay about the misunderstood marsupial on these pages) and Dunlap has not only painted one, he is the creator of the tasty opossum cocktail (vodka, a splash of cranberry juice, a dash or two of orange bitters, and an orange slice as garnish). As a prop of sorts (and perhaps a spot of inspiration), we decided to bring the cocktails with us onto the "stage," which was actually the chancel of a Methodist church that had been commandeered for the occasion.

As it happened, a few months before the event, Mississippi governor Phil Bryant had signed a bill into law that allowed handguns inside churches. For an added flourish, Bryant chose to do so with his own personal handgun, a Glock, atop the large family Bible on his desk, a newspaper image greeted with an alarming amount of equanimity by a large segment of the populace. Roy and Dunlap and I, on the other hand, did not fare so well with the locals. Weeks after our panel, we learned we'd caused something of a scandal for drinking alcohol in the Methodist sanctuary. Too bad we weren't packing heat instead. No one would have flinched.

This is the kind of stuff that keeps you pretty much constantly on your toes. It also provides ample fodder for people like me who make a living documenting the various goings-on in these environs. The particular goings-on in this volume were all penned for *Garden & Gun* magazine, where I've been writing since its happy inception more than a decade ago. Its very name is a juxtaposition, taken from a fabled, sadly long-shuttered bar in Charleston, South Carolina, where I was lucky enough to be taken as an underage college student visiting the city for a friend's debutante party. There were ceiling fans and balconies, sailors and socialites, the occasional drag queen and the frequent sockless Gucci wearer. It was an eclectic, high-low mix of folks, one not entirely representative of the South, but close enough that the founders of a magazine about Southern culture chose to take its name.

My column in the magazine is called, appropriately, "The High & The Low" and I have a great time brainstorming its wide-ranging topics with my intrepid editor, David DiBennedetto. I write about our music and our food (two of the region's best gifts to the rest of the country), our critters (and our penchant for hunting and making a meal of them), our drinking habits (prodigious), our talent for making our own fun (highly necessary), and some of our more embarrassing tendencies (including our seemingly bottomless propensity for committing a whole lot of craziness in the name of the Lord). I still get mighty embarrassed by the behavior of some of the folks in my region, but it also has been my fellow Southerners who have brought me the greatest joy—on the page, over the airwaves, around the dinner table, at the bar or, hell, in the checkout line.

Willie contended he could best write about the land of our birth from the distance Manhattan afforded him. I find it useful—and endlessly entertaining—to be right here in the thick of things. What I love most about where I live is that my fellow residents have always had an enormous capacity for laughing at themselves—for good reason, of course, but it's a quality we could all do with a lot more of in these fraught times. It's hot and even more humid, the mosquitoes are murderous, and we might all be half crazy, but I am grateful every day that I ended up returning South toward home.

Part One

Personal Notes

Grace Under Pressure

"FUNCTION IN DISASTER, FINISH IN STYLE" IS ONE OF THE
mottoes of the Madeira School, the all-girls boarding school in
McLean, Virginia, where I happily spent my junior and senior
years. *Festina lente* ("Make haste slowly") is the official motto,
the one engraved on our class rings, but as anyone who knows
me can tell you, that's not really my thing. I prefer the informal
one, the one that was drummed into the student body by Lucy
Madeira Wing, who founded the school in 1906, ten years
after she graduated from Vassar. When my mother was at Madeira in the 1950s, Miss Madeira was still alive and pretty
much kicking and she delivered the line to the assembled girls
almost every morning.

I have been thinking about Miss Madeira and her guiding
principle a lot lately. Perhaps because so few in our midst seem to
be living by it. On a particularly bad summer day this past summer, for example, I was driving from the Hartford, Connecticut,

airport to the Vermont graduation of my good friend Ellen's son, late and speeding (in defiance of the charge of the ring on my little finger), and listening to an especially incessant drumbeat of doom on NPR. My friend and favorite senator from Mississippi, a total class act and by far the best advocate for our poor state, was under siege from a primary challenger whom I'll refrain from characterizing here in a Herculean effort to be a class act myself. War was escalating in so many places at once I was reminded of my Madeira Modern European History class and the lectures of the good Dr. Brown on the events leading up to World War I. A particular wing of the Republican Party seemed not to have taken even an elementary school civics class, much less modern history of any kind, and the administration was, well, being the administration.

The center does not hold, I thought. Common sense does not prevail. No one is functioning in disaster, much less finishing with a modicum of style. But then I made it to the graduation at the Burr Burton Academy atop a gorgeous green hill. The young women and men were all dressed up beneath their caps and gowns—my friend's son, the handsome Eli, wore a fetching pale orange button-down shirt, a green tie, and a conservative but well-cut poplin suit. The leadership award was won by two beautiful girls who were best friends. The valedictorian talked about responsibility, integrity, service, and grit (grit!). And the speaker, a case study in Miss Madeira's mantra, was Kevin Pearce, the snowboarder who suffered a traumatic brain injury and had to learn not just how to walk and talk again, but also how to swallow and brush his teeth. Now, he runs the Kevin Pearce Fund to help people with injuries like his. He told the kids he was "living proof you can overcome what you've been dealt," that they should "focus on this moment and be proud."

So we all did and we all were. We went to dinner at the nearby Downtown Grocery, owned by my fellow Mississippian Abby Coker and her husband, the brilliant chef Rogan Lechthaler. We had delicious rhubarb margaritas, bought a round of Miller ponies for the kitchen staff (per Abby's menu instructions if we liked what we ate—and we loved it all), lit sparklers at the table, and generally had a huge warm time.

Pretty much everybody that day had finished in style, and it made me realize once again that the best center to hold is your own. Which brings me back to Miss Madeira. Her simple definition of education was "discipline of the mind," and I can tell you that in my two years at her school I worked and thought harder than I ever have since. She agreed with Robert Louis Stevenson's opinion that the world had best hurry up and return to the "word duty and be done with the word reward." She decreed that there would be no class rankings and grades would not be posted. She taught the public affairs and Bible courses herself (in my day, the latter had morphed into ethics, but a close friend who took that small and intense class ended up with a Ph.D. in theology and ministered to folks at a church near Ground Zero on 9/11).

My mother remembers that Miss Madeira was wild about the young queen Elizabeth and implored the girls to emulate not just her "dignity and quiet poise" but her proper low-heeled English shoes. "She hated the Capezio flats we all wore," my mother says, adding that she thought them "sloppy." Miss Madeira, described by *Time* in 1946 as "one of Washington's last New Dealers," told the magazine that she regretted the fact that most of her students came from "economic royalist" families and put them all in the same outfits lest they try to outspend each other. In spring, my mother reports, the girls dressed in green jumpers with white cotton blouses, while in winter it was the same blouse with a gray skirt and a yellow or green sweater. For dinner they changed into white piqué dresses, and in the senior portraits of my mother's yearbook, every single girl has on a string of pearls.

I arrived well after the era of white piqué, in time to enjoy the hangover of the far more lax rules of the sixties, which would come to an abrupt end almost as soon as I left the gates. We had no adult supervision in our dorms and elected our own dorm mothers from our peers. We smoked pot in the woods and cigarettes on the outdoor smoking terrace or in the unspeakably grungy senior clubhouse. I kept a fifth of Scotch in my underwear drawer, and one of my dorm mates was in possession of a blender with which we made the occasional birthday daiquiri. The queen, who is now among my own heroines, was not much on our radar screens.

The equitable Miss Madeira would have been appalled at the charge accounts we had with the local taxi service, which we sent on runs for Häagen-Dazs and Chinese takeout (accompanied by six-packs of Tsingtao beer). A great many of us got around the lone dress code requirement of a skirt at dinner by wrapping our plaid gym kilts around whatever we were already wearing, which in my case was usually a pair of Levi's pulled over the Lanz nightgown in which I awoke—the only outfit that would enable me to make it to chapel (barely) on time.

Looking back, the best I can hope for is that Miss Madeira would have perhaps been gratified that it was still impossible to tell anything about the wealth and class of most of us by our appearance—we all looked equally awful. (In our defense, some of the staff didn't look a whole lot better—the school nurse was fond of combing mayonnaise through her steel-gray hair.) The only exceptions were the Carolina girls who wore wraparound skirts and the same cotton shirts of my mother's era with gold clip-on earrings, add-a-bead necklaces, and Pappagallo flats or Weejuns. When I met my roommate, who hailed from Wadesboro, North Carolina, for the first time, I was wearing my favorite Adidas T-shirt, ancient Levi's, and a pair of Earth shoes. She walked in with neatly coiffed hair and mascara, trailed by her brother, who was carrying, I swear, a crate of African violets for our windowsills. I ended up loving her, and, I think, she me, but I never saw the point of wasting time trying to pull myself together—except, of course, on Wednesdays.

Wednesdays were the days when we were bused into town for internships. In our junior year we all worked on Capitol Hill; in our senior year, we were supposed to know what we wanted to be when we grew up, so I worked at the Washington bureau of *Newsweek*, then owned by Katharine Graham, a Madeira alum who totally got the hang of our founder's dictum. On those days, the style we most emulated was that of a thirty-five-year-old—the better to enable us to order martinis during our lunch breaks. So dramatically different was my own appearance that when I ran into my photography teacher in Lafayette Park, he had no idea who I was.

Let me pause and say here that I am not necessarily proud of some aspects of my school career. And I should hasten to reassure prospective Madeira parents that I would have lasted about an hour and a half under the current school rules. It's a miracle I lasted then—when I attended a school function a year after graduation, the dean of students, Jean Gisriel (known universally as Miss Giz), stuck her formidable face about two inches in front of mine and said, with a mixture of profound disgust and surprisingly raw frustration, "I never could get you. I never could."

Still, Miss Giz and the rest of our leaders (with the notable exception of Jean Harris, the murderous headmistress who arrived my senior year) managed to instill Miss Madeira's core beliefs into us all. And the school itself is a prime example of holding it together in the direst of circumstances. After Mrs. Harris was arrested for shooting her ex-lover the Scarsdale Diet doctor, Herman Tarnower, almost every newspaper in the country identified her as the headmistress of the "posh" Madeira School. My mother was appalled, and fears were rife that applications would all but cease. But my father, as usual, got it on the money: "Every redneck in America is going to want to send their kid to that 'posh' place." Sure enough, applications surged.

The school is still all girls and still thriving, and I am forever grateful for my time there and what it taught me. Not least of which is how to hold on tight and fake it during those trying stretches when functioning—and finishing—are not necessarily assured. To that end, I will repeat the line I chose for my senior yearbook page, not from Miss Madeira, but from Andrew Jackson: "You are uneasy; you've never sailed with me before, I see."

New Year, Old Habits

EVERY NEW YEAR I MEET FRIENDS AT MY MOTHER'S HOUSE in Seaside, Florida. On New Year's Eve I make Lee Bailey's Pasta with Golden Caviar and on New Year's Day I make black-eyed peas with andouille, and on both occasions we drink lavish amounts of Veuve Clicquot provided by my great pals Joyce and Rod, who are possessed of a seemingly bottomless cache. Then, on January 2, pretty much everybody in town packs up and moves out, leaving the dog and me to get on with the real business at hand: my annual attempt at accomplishing two very important missions. The missions stay the same because I never actually accomplish them. What happens instead is that I reread all the John D. MacDonald and Robert B. Parker paperbacks in the house, sleep, walk the dog, and sleep some more. But I digress.

Back to the missions. First I endeavor to find inner peace and learn to breathe by booking a massage every day and signing up for yoga, a practice in which I last engaged the summer before my fortieth birthday, well over a decade ago. Last year I got as far as the first massage. The masseuse rubbed some oil on her hands and then she stroked my face and told me to "let go of all that which does not serve you." This woman is really, really nice and gives one of the best massages I've ever had, but in the immortal words of my friend Rick Smythe, "Naw, that ain't gonna happen." And it certainly is not going to happen in ninety minutes, or even in ten ninety-minute sessions. When I finally stopped laughing, I got completely freaked out by all the stuff I tote around in my head and heart that does me absolutely no good, and then I realized it wasn't even a metaphor.

Which leads me to the second mission: to go through the ever burgeoning amount of actual tote bags containing all the work I meant to finish, mail I meant to answer, and magazine articles I meant to read during the previous twelve months (although at this point, it's really more like seventy-two). Last year, I took a whopping eleven bags with me and then I brought them all back home. Currently, they are stashed beneath the desk at which I am typing, ready to be reloaded into the car for the annual trip. In 2009, I left a particularly heavy bag in my Seaside bedroom with the firm intention of coming *right back* and dealing with it. I didn't, of course, and now I have no idea what's inside, but on top there's a September 1998 *New York Review of Books* with a cover story on Elizabeth Hardwick by Joyce Carol Oates, which means that I've been carrying it around for fifteen years and three months. It would take me maybe twenty minutes to read the essay, but now it's become a Thing, a reminder of my almost pathological procrastination and countless other inadequacies and of Oates's own terrifying productivity. She has written seventy-eight pieces for the *New York Review*; I have written two. She is also the author of more than forty novels and a whole bunch of poems and short stories, none of which I have read, and she also teaches. At Princeton.

So this year, I'm changing the plan. I'm going to read the damn Joyce Carol Oates story and then I'm going to dump out the remaining contents of the bag and all the other bags too. If I weren't sure I'd be breaking some town ordinance, I would set fire to it all. Next I'm going to dump out the electronic tote bag that is my email inbox, in which I have 25,652 new messages. A few months ago they were down to a modest 4,000, but then my computer got hacked and the nice man in India to whom I paid five hundred dollars to retrieve my lost emails retrieved every single one I'd received since 2008. At first I was going to make them another mission—I'd go through all the missives from the past two or three years and respond. Because when I get an email, unless it's a life-threatening one from one of my editors, including the fearless (and astonishingly patient) leader of the magazine for which I write these columns, I rarely reply. What I think is this: "Man, I need to take more than two seconds to craft an answer, so I'll save it and jump back on it in just a little bit," and then I never do.

I have lost out on potentially lucrative speaking engagements and festive parties and made a whole lot of people mad or at least a little perplexed. This week, for example, I ran into a very nice man, an orthopedic surgeon from Chattanooga who gently reminded me that I'd failed to respond to the email he'd sent two years earlier asking for my grillades recipe. Naturally,

I didn't remember the email or even the brunch I'd given where he'd tasted the grillades in question. This was a screw-up of many dimensions. First of all, it's always good to have a top-notch ortho man in your list of contacts. You never know when or where you might break a leg. Also, it would have been, at a minimum, polite of me to get back to him. Finally, since I often write about food for a living, it's not a bad thing to have people in various cities around the country talking about the tastiness of my grillades.

So, in this space, I'm answering his email. As for the rest of you, sorry, but I'm deleting all the others. Then I'm making two resolutions. I'm going to answer my email. When it comes in. And I'm throwing out all my tote bags. If I don't have them, I can't fill them up.

Grillades

SERVES 8

Seasoning mix

> 1 tbsp. salt
> 1½ tsp. onion powder
> 1½ tsp. garlic powder
> 1½ tsp. cayenne
> 1 tsp. white pepper
> 1 tsp. sweet paprika
> 1 tsp. black pepper
> ½ tsp. dry mustard
> ½ tsp. dried thyme
> ½ tsp. gumbo filé

For the Grillades

2 lbs. boneless veal or pork shoulder, cut into thin
slices

1 cup all-purpose flour

7 tbsp. vegetable oil

1 cup chopped onions

1 cups chopped celery

1 cup chopped green bell peppers

2 tsp. minced garlic

4 bay leaves

3 cups dark chicken, veal, or beef stock

½ cup red wine

1½ cups canned whole peeled tomatoes, drained and
torn into pieces

1 tbsp. Worcestershire sauce

1 tsp. dried thyme

Preparation

Combine the seasoning mix ingredients in a small bowl.
Sprinkle about 2 teaspoons of the mix on both sides of the
meat. In a sheet pan, combine ½ half cup of the flour with another teaspoon of seasoning mix. Dredge the meat in the flour
shaking off excess. Heat the oil in a large deep skillet or Dutch
oven and fry the meat until golden brown about two or three
minutes per side. Transfer the meat to a plate or another sheet
pan and leave the oil in the skillet over high heat.

Sprinkle in the remaining half cup of flour, whisking
constantly. Continue whisking until the roux is a medium
brown, about three minutes. Immediately dump in the chopped

vegetables and stir with a wooden spoon until well blended. Add the bay leaves and another two teaspoons of seasoning mix. Continue cooking about five minutes, stirring constantly.

Add stock to the vegetable mixture, stirring until well incorporated. Add the meat, wine, tomatoes, Worcestershire sauce, and thyme and bring to a boil. Reduce to a simmer and cook for about 40 minutes. Midway through, check for seasonings. You will have some seasoning mix left over, and you may add to taste. Serve hot, with cheese grits.

Songs of Summer

IN THE SUMMER OF 1969, RICHARD NIXON'S FIRST ONE AS president, my father was appointed to the American Revolution Bicentennial Commission (the Mississippi delegation had supported Nixon's nomination at the Republican National Convention the previous summer, and Nixon was a grateful man). The first meeting was, fittingly, in July, so my mother decided to come too and take my first cousin Frances and me to see the nation's capital. Frances was two months older than I was—which meant she was already nine and I was eight—but in terms of cool she was light-years ahead. She was taller and thinner and wore her long hair parted in the middle (my mother was forever pulling mine back with a gold barrette). Frances owned a beautiful chestnut pony named Key Biscayne; I rode a fat white mare belonging to my riding teacher, who called her Mary Poppins. On the plane from Nashville, where Frances lived, we wore matching white piqué Florence Eiseman dresses, but mine was accessorized by a lame red, white, and blue scarf in keeping with the spirit of the outing. Frances's scarf had been designed by über-hip pop artist Peter Max and was a gift from the impossibly gorgeous and twenty-years-younger man Frances's mother, my aunt Frances, would later marry.

Anyway, even though we had just completed the third grade, Frances was, naturally, up on everything, including the songs on that summer's pop charts. Her two favorites were: "Ruby, Don't Take Your Love to Town," the (upon grown-up reflection) antiwar song about a paralyzed vet and his philandering woman, written by the great Mel Tillis and made famous by Kenny Rogers and the First Edition; and "Spinning Wheel," the horn-heavy and comparatively psychedelic tune by Blood, Sweat & Tears.

It was a fun trip. We had a private tour of the White House, climbed the stairs to the top of the Washington Monument, and were allowed to assist the pretty young woman who ran the gift shop at our hotel, the newly opened Madison. But what I remember most were those two songs and every single one of their lyrics, which Frances sang pretty much nonstop. She sang them to the tourists while my mother paddled us in a boat around the Tidal Basin; she sang them from the backseat during the entire car ride to Colonial Williamsburg. I am confident that my mother still shudders at the sound of the opening chord of each, but to me they will forever be symbols of that summer and how much I adored my now departed cousin.

I mourn Frances every day, but I also mourn those time-specific singles that would become the anthems and/or background music of each season. They were like the lead characters in Don Henley's addictive "Boys of Summer": You know they're coming, you can't wait for their arrival, they mark your experience like nothing else, and then they're gone. Songs are still released every summer, of course, but unless they were played on one of the three channels I listen to most on SiriusXM, I couldn't possibly tell you which ones were most popular last year. But without looking it up, I can tell you right now that Bonnie Raitt's "Something to Talk About" was released in May 1991—it was my first, very memorable, summer in New Orleans and I was up to the same thing she was.

The thing—and the shame—is, it could be my song again this summer, and so, for that matter, could "Ruby" (though I think I'll pass). On any given day I can listen to either or both on my laptop, my phone, or in my new car that's tricked out with Sirius and Pandora and God knows what else (I have yet to read the manual). But if the songs of summer can be whatever you want them to be, those three supercharged months—marked by freedom and possibility and some life-changing moment of love or lust or longing for something you might not even know yet—won't be nearly as vividly defined or so accurately placed in time. I want (need) a song to immediately dial up what I wore and whom I loved, what I drove and what I dreamed about. A sound track lends even potentially fleeting moments an indelible quality not unlike a movie scene. The songs meant that everybody had a reel.

Herewith I offer a handful of highlights from my own reel, which, with a notable exception, makes an excellent summer playlist:

"Band of Gold"

FREDA PAYNE

It's 1970 in Nashville. I shuttle between my grandparents' house and that of Aunt Frances, who is not much focused on her children during that summer. Frances and I spend most nights on cots from the Army-Navy store in what was once our back-yard dollhouse, smoking cadged Maryland 100s cigarettes and burning incense to mask the smell. We have a hip new digital clock radio and roll the dial back and forth between WMAK and WKDA. "Ride Captain Ride" is Frances's favorite and I don't dare tell her I think it might be the worst song ever re-corded. Instead, I can't get enough of the seriously great "Band of Gold," the favorite of Ernestine Turner, my grandmother's cook, who I adore at least as much as Frances. We run errands in Ernestine's Chevy Nova and sing it at the top of our lungs, along with Joe Cocker's excellent version of "The Letter" from the same summer (Ernestine, having ditched her husband, and her own band of gold, is now dating a postman). Thirty-two years later, I'm lucky enough to be a guest at Liza Minelli's ill-fated wedding to the late producer David Gest. Since he specialized in comeback acts, the reception's musical guests (Petula Clark, the surviving members of the Fifth Dimension, B.J. Thomas, the reunited Doobie Brothers, Billy Paul) play what is essentially a list of the songs of summers past, including "Band of Gold," sung by Freda herself. I shed a tear for Ernestine and cannot believe my luck.

"Mercy Me (The Ecology)"

MARVIN GAYE

It's 1971 and Aunt Frances has married the man who is now my Uncle Mike. He drives a vintage forest green Mercedes (the first I'd ever seen) and his presence in our family ups Frances's cool quotient even higher. When "Mercy Me," which spends two weeks at the top of the August charts, comes on the radio, he explains to us what the word "ecology" means. We are enthralled.

"Cowgirl in the Sand"/"Love the One You're With"

CROSBY, STILLS, NASH & YOUNG

It's 1974 and Crosby, Stills, Nash & Young have reunited for an epic tour. By now I have my own stereo and I'm especially in love with Stephen Stills and Neil Young. Frances is visiting us in Mississippi and we convince my mother to take us to Memphis with my best friend Jessica to see CSN&Y perform in a stadium that no longer exists. Spoiled, protected, and ridiculously bourgeois, we manage to fill a thermos with Kahlua, the only booze on my parents' bar we knew they wouldn't miss. We'd not yet become acquainted with the recreational drugs we saw the folks around us partaking of, but in our huaraches and gauze Indian shirts, we hoped desperately that we fit in. Jesse Colin Young and Santana opened and it remains one of the best concerts I've ever seen.

"Muskrat Love"

CAPTAIN & TENNILLE

It's the summer of 1976, a month before another Republican National Convention is going to decide between President Gerald Ford and Ronald Reagan, former governor of California. Mississippi is the last uncommitted delegation and my father, its chairman, is a mighty popular man. He and my mother are invited to the White House for the State Dinner in honor of Queen Elizabeth and Prince Philip, which is not, I assure you, the reason why he ultimately cast his vote for Ford. My mother, who is wearing a diamond necklace my grandmother has sent in a box on the bus from Nashville, sits next to Bill Blass and gives Cary Grant directions to the loo. The dinner is in a tent over the Rose Garden and the menu features California wines, New England lobster, and a peach ice cream bombe. Everything is perfect except, unbelievably, Captain and Tennille have been asked to entertain. I cannot imagine what the queen made of this song, complete with the synthesizer sound effects of the muskrats mating.

"Too Long at the Fair"

BONNIE RAITT

Bonnie's second album came out in the summer of 1972, but it doesn't have pride of place in my eight-track tape deck until the summer of 1976, my first behind the wheel of a car. Every song is perfect (including Jackson Browne's "Under the Falling

Sky"), but this one best conjures the lost love and heartbreak the aforementioned Jessica and I both thought we'd already suffered. It would be awhile before we knew the real thing, but in the meantime we could throw back the top of my navy 1967 Mustang convertible, crank up Bonnie, and drown our overblown teenage sorrows with an under-age six-pack of Miller ponies.

"Miss You"

THE ROLLING STONES

This song is released in May 1978, the same month I graduate from high school and is played on an almost continual loop at the late and much lamented One Block East, one of the world's greatest ever bars. My male running buddies and I play a happy hour drinking game that involves a pitcher of beer, a lit cigarette, and a dime, and take great pleasure in mimicking Mick's high-pitched chorus. Eleven years later, I'm about to get married and the same gang offers to reprise the song as an all-too-fitting recessional in the church. That's not why I end up calling off the wedding, but the cancellation coincides with my favorite song of that particular summer (1989), Mary Chapin Carpenter's "Quitting Time." Most people treat me like I have a brain tumor (*Newsweek* has just come out with a cover citing a study saying women who aren't married by age thirty have a greater chance of being killed by a terrorist than tying the knot—and this is when there weren't many terrorists). Meanwhile, I'm juking up and down the streets of Manhattan with "Quitting Time" on my Walkman. The one person who articulates what I felt—better, even, than Carpenter—is my father's good friend John Alsop. When I call him with the news, he says, simply, "Relief's a hell of an emotion, isn't it?" Yep, it is. Every time I hear that song, I still feel a refreshing surge of it, and every time I hear "Miss You," I crack up over the vision of that motley would-be nuptial choir. It's great to be both seventeen and twenty-eight again. I remember exactly how it felt.

Stuff, Sweet Stuff

About three weeks before my now ex-husband and I were slated to close on our New Orleans house, I thought it might be a good idea to take a gander inside our storage unit—the one we'd rented nine years earlier, the one where we'd stashed a ton of stuff while we endured the tortuous renovation of the Greek Revival pile we were selling, the one I figured must still be chock-full because otherwise, why had we been paying for it once a month every month for all that time? It was not full, not even close. Instead, it contained: six boxes of birds' nests, two carrying cases of cassette tapes, a broken vase, four boxes of magazines, and, most thrillingly, a Carolina Herrera cocktail dress still inside the shipping carton from my former Manhattan drycleaner Madame Paulette.

Looking at all that space, my first thought was, naturally, "You idiot." And then there was the slightly unsettling time capsule nature of things. The mix-tapes I couldn't bear to give up had been rendered obsolete by my iPod Nano (invented in 2005). The magazines (*House & Garden*, *Southern Accents*, *Vogue Living*, *Domino*) that had served as inspiration for so much of the house's décor were no longer in print. The dress, a thing of beauty adorned with black feathers, had last graced my body ten years earlier, at my rehearsal dinner. But as interesting (and, in the case of the magazines, bittersweet) as the discoveries may have been, my main emotion was relief. Though I'd secured a rather vast temporary apartment from which to ponder my next move, I knew I would still need that mostly empty unit. For one thing, I'd already managed to collect a great many more birds' nests.

Here's the thing I've learned: Houses and apartments come and go, but your stuff is, well, your stuff. For example, some of the *House & Gardens* in the box date from 1980, the year I had my first solo apartment, near Washington's Dupont Circle. Since then, I've lived in at least eight more places, all influenced at least a little bit by the stacks of magazines I move from place to place, and by the ever-increasing amounts of possessions, from books to birds' nests, I've acquired.

Lots of words have been written about home being where your heart, your love, your dog, your parakeet, whatever, is. I get it—bricks and mortar don't make a home and all that jazz (though if the Waterworks Empire tub I'm leaving behind in my bathroom counts as bricks and mortar, then it was well worth the investment). For me, home is where you find the touchstones of your life: the yellow and white "wedding" china that was a gift from my grandfather prior to nuptials that never happened; the John Alexander portrait of my noble cat Sam (and his ashes that are somewhere in the armoire that holds the sheets); the giant tortoiseshell I smuggled out of Grenada during a hilariously hellish cruise with my dear departed cousin Frances and our grandfather. And then there are the nests: the nest of the weaverbird I smuggled out of Tanzania much to my mother's profound horror (and fear—she refused to come anywhere near me at customs in Atlanta), the rare Carolina warbler nest my friend Bobby Harling's sweet father found for me still attached to the branch. I have an odd connection to these nests (especially since messing with them as a child earned me a bout with histoplasmosis). They are beautiful and heroic (I mean talk about daunting construction problems) and I'm sure a shrink could make much of their symbolism regarding my own nesting needs. But I'm actually a bit of a vagabond—I just need to know I can take my nests with me when I go.

And that's the thing about touchstones: unlike a house, you can take them with you. After all, generations of Southerners have made a semiprofession out of toting around and lavishly tending to family heirlooms and prized possessions—though that's not exactly what I have in mind. The only family portrait I have is of a relative so stern and scary no one else would take her, and while (note to my mother) I am wildly grateful for the generous amounts of silver sent my way, I am even more crazy about the handsome bronze bear that once sat on my grandmother's back hall telephone table and the countless porcelain ashtrays where she rested her steady stream of Pall Malls. Recently I came across my great-grandfather's caramel leather suitcase, the back of which I used as a headboard of sorts while lying in my grandmother's luggage room, reading books deemed unsuitable for my age. A garret off the tiny but much-trafficked bar, the luggage room also afforded frequent visits to the mini fridge where I gorged myself on martini garnishes and monitored the ever diminishing contents of the label-less vodka bottle refilled by the houseman, Louis King, every morning. Proust had his madeleines—pimento stuffed olives and cocktail onions will forever be my own.

If I seriously miss any house at hall, it would have to be my grandmother's, with its vast basement and warm laundry smell, the formica kitchen table where Louis taught me five-card stud, the elevator where Frances and I hid out and smoked. I will miss the house we sold too, of course. It was lovely and light-filled and possessed of its own memories and life-altering events, the first couple of years of which I put down in a book. But the thing about doing that, about writing a fairly personal book about your house and the road that led to acquiring it, means that everyone who read it thinks it's their business when you sell it. "Why?" was the chorus as soon as we'd hung out the sign.

The most tempting rejoinder was, of course, *"None ya"* but there are plenty of reasons. There was the fact that I'd accumulated at least four more boxes full of house mags in the eight years we resided there and I was antsy for a new project. There was the murderous rage that was reignited almost every time I ripped my hand open on the multiple flayed doorknob screws courtesy of my disastrous contractor or came across some similar gift from him that would clearly never quit giving. Mostly, though, there was the instinct to jump off a cliff, shake things up, take a step or two back before the house itself became too much of its own thing, for lack of a better word.

It had taken on so much importance, with its own timetable and demands, that I began to feel like a curator. Though we had a trillion parties, we never had the glam official house-warming bash I'd always envisioned because I was waiting to "finish," something I finally understood would never, ever, happen.

Then, of course, there was the very real responsibility of the endless hedge trimming (so big and damnably healthy my tree man asked me if I was feeding them chickens), of replacing the forever burnt-out fountain pumps, of fighting the termites and the leaf miners and the buckmoth caterpillars falling like little bombs from the live oaks—not to mention the bees (!) who took up very expensive residence in the columns on our front porch. The week before we finally closed, the bedroom ceiling fell in, another consequence of the aforementioned contractor and his moronic AC man, who long ago wound something the wrong way causing years of steady condensation that finally rotted through the lathes, the plaster, and two layers of Sheetrock as a parting gift.

When that happened, I was reminded of my friend the antiques dealer Peter Patout, who once woke up and rearranged his furniture (beautifully) in the middle of the night. When I asked him what had possessed him to get out of bed and start moving the settees around, he shot back, "Jesus told me to" with a (sort of) straight face. That really should have been my answer to my neighbors: Jesus was clearly telling us to get the hell out of the house as fast as we possibly could. The same day the ceiling collapsed, the paper had a big piece about an incurable citrus virus that might well kill all of Louisiana's trees, and I swear my lime tree was afflicted.

So we left, with all our respective stuff in tow. I toted off the nests and what seemed like a thousand boxes of books, the cat's ashes and my grandmother's ashtrays and the mangy boar's head everyone kept telling me to leave on the street. It is the same stuff that will land in the next house, and wherever it may turn out to be, I think I'll go on and have the housewarming the first week. I need a place to wear that feathered dress again and I can decorate with all the nests. I do love a theme.

Say What?

I HAVE MADE MY LIVING AS A WRITER FOR MORE THAN thirty years, and in all that time, the comment I've gotten most is "You write just like you talk." I choose to take this as a compliment, to believe that what people mean is that I sound (dare I say it) authentic and relatively accessible without too many airs. This is what you strive for, what is called in the trade a "voice," a slightly heightened version of your actual self. Once, early on, when I was trying perhaps too hard to adhere to the old-fashioned newsman rule of "who, what, when, where, and why" (which never, ever, involved the first person), an editor scrawled in the margins of my story, "Where are YOU??" These days one might well make the case that I am all too present in my prose. But there is one thing I now know for sure. I might have a voice, but I do not write like I talk.

I made this discovery in September 2015 when I broke my left elbow while crossing one of New Orleans' typically mean streets. The first (not so hot) doctor set my arm in a hard cast for several weeks, a course of action that turned out to be entirely unnecessary or just flat-out wrong, depending on who you talk to. Worse, my palm was facing up so that I looked like a perpetual waitress, albeit one no good for passing anything other than a very small plate of airy hors d'oeuvres. You'd be amazed at what you need two arms (and hands) for. At one point, on a visit to New York, I had to ask the startled night porter at the University Club to unzip me. What neither the porter nor anyone else could do for me was my job, though almost to a man, everybody I encountered cheerfully insisted that I was lucky, that today's smart technology would see me through. "Don't worry," they said. "That's what your dictation app is for. It won't be a problem."

It was a problem. First of all, like the iPhone's highly temperamental Siri, Dragon and the rest of the dictation apps I tried steadfastly refused to understand pretty much everything I had to say. Dragon's trademarked slogan is "NaturallySpeaking," but apparently none of its coders have spent a natural minute below the Mason-Dixon Line. A smart person could make a lot of money by inventing a Siri for Southerners (and maybe for French folks too). Each time I sent an email asking someone to meet me at Cochon, one of my favorite local restaurants, it came out "kosher," a supremely ironic substitution considering that Cochon, as the name implies, is a shrine to slaughtered pig meat. When my friend the artist Bill Dunlap dictates an email to me, it invariably begins, "Dear Junior." Now he calls me Junior all the time, and it's funny. What is not funny is the fact that the only words my computer unfailingly recognized were the epithets I hurled at its screen, where whole lines of them would dutifully appear. Which meant that I'd have to use my good hand to erase them and start all over again.

All that cussing and deleting and stopping and starting can really slow down, if not entirely derail, a train of thought. But even on the rare occasions when things would go smoothly for a whole paragraph at a time, I finally realized it was no good. I couldn't even blame the technology. While I'd have appreciated better cooperation on those emails, it turns out that I cannot talk a story. Dictation is better suited for the "just the facts, ma'am" lingo of lawyers and doctors, for whom Dragon was developed. I once threw an orange at my ex-husband for using "pretermit" in normal conversation. Clearly he had been dictating too many lawyerly documents for too long. My own so-called voice is not my literal voice, which is a result of lungs and larynx and all manner of other speech organs working together to enable a sound to make contact. It is a rather more hard-won thing that comes, finally, from putting pen to paper or fingers to keys.

When we talk, we rarely edit ourselves, as anyone (which is to say everyone) who has ever regretted a word that flew out of his or her mouth knows. We tend, as well, to drone on, especially in the South, a place famous for what scholars like to call our "oral tradition." Loosely translated, this means that we are prone to drink a lot of whiskey and spin a lot of yarns. And since we started out in a rural, mostly agricultural place, no one had anything better to do than gather round and listen. I've done plenty of this myself, usually in bars rather than on the fabled front porch. I once spent almost seven hours with Dunlap, who also happens to be a good writer, in Galatoire's. We consumed at least a case of wine and carried on what we persisted in thinking was the kind of conversation that would solve everything, the kind that Hemingway (who was drunk himself a whole lot of the time) would rather pompously describe as "true." Of course, neither of us could remember a shred of it the next day. The thing about the oral tradition is that it's mostly enjoyable for the talkers. And it helps if everyone within hearing distance is drunk too. (Hemingway also said, "I drink to make other people more interesting.") With few exceptions (Winston Churchill, William F. Buckley, Jr., my old pal Christopher Hitchens), most of us don't talk remotely as agilely or as thoughtfully as we write. Even Jerry Clower did not just get on the radio or TV and yack. He wrote all that seemingly off-the-cuff cornpone humor down first.

With that, I shall write down my own story. Mainly because I got tired of answering the question "How drunk were you?" This was closely followed by "How bad did you hurt him?" (My acquaintances imagine themselves to be at least as amusing as Clower himself.) First, I was not drunk and I didn't hit anybody, though I really, really wanted to. It was morning, I'd been working, I was taking my dog, Henry, out for what I thought would be a quick walk. But then we ran into the cemetery tourists. I live across from Lafayette No. 1, a bedraggled, constantly crumbling aboveground graveyard that out-of-towners cannot seem to get enough of. Despite all the post-Katrina hoopla about New Orleans' newly diversified economy, it remains largely tourist based, so we're exhorted to be pleasant to our visitors. I try mightily, but on this particular morning an irritating couple waiting for their tour guide made a beeline for Henry, who is, admittedly, irresistible, and proceeded to mess with his ears. Henry is a social animal—if the Orkin man, say, were to walk through the door, he'd run around in circles, jump on and off every piece of nearby furniture, mewl and bark, and go into a general paroxysm of joy. But on the street, he tends toward reticence. So I cut the visit short and yanked him away, at which point the predators began to make a fuss about how cruel I was being to my dog. Clearly, they'd never walked a beagle, an ongoing ballet of pushes and pulls, yanks and coaxings, and anyway, I couldn't be mean to Henry if I tried hard. So now I was stomping mad and in the middle of the street when some newly formed asphalt protrusion launched me like a missile. Henry was not only unhurt, he was too busy sniffing to notice. I knew I was not so lucky, which made me madder still. Apparently the tourists do not spend enough money for the city to do basic things like pave the streets, which are not unlike those of Afghanistan, where I have been. (They also don't make us enough money to replace the four hundred cops we've lost in the last five years. If you don't fall down, you might get shot instead, but I digress.)

After a couple of months of trial and error, I found a South African miracle worker in Manhattan named David Helfet. My elbow was fixed and I could type and I only had to wear a sling for a week after the virtually painless surgery. Plus, it was not a brain tumor or anything else a really smart Afrikaner couldn't ultimately fix with a couple of screws and a plate, so I'm lucky. I was also reminded, at this advanced stage of my career, of the importance of putting pen to actual paper. Some of my best writing has always been on the back of vomit bags on airplanes—I'm not kidding—and I was forced to resort to this again (though mostly on a legal pad). I can hear, suspended in the air, the rhythm of my voice—my slowed-down, already edited voice—telling me what to write, quick, before I forget it, so I usually reach for the closest thing to hand.

Shelby Foote wrote six novels, countless letters (notably to his closest friend, Walker Percy), and his unsurpassed three-volume *The Civil War: A Narrative* in longhand with an ink pen, a real one he called a "dip pen" because you had to repeatedly dip it in a pot of ink. During that one twenty-year project, he put more than a million words on paper, but he didn't mind. In fact, he felt it was crucial. He told an interviewer, "I like the feel that a pen or pencil gives you, being in close touch with the paper and with nothing mechanical between you and it. The very notion of a word processor horrifies me." I can only imagine his horror at Siri and the rest, but it would be a moot point. No dictation app on the planet could have made sense of Foote's courtly Deep South cadences, and the world is better for it.

I'm with the Band

THE OTHER DAY I RAN INTO A RELATIVELY NEW FRIEND of mine at one of my favorite New Orleans restaurants, Lilette, and when he introduced me to his tablemates, he told the story of our first meeting. He was clearer than I on the details, which went something like this: We were at the same museum gala, there was good food and good music, and during the course of our conversation I asked if he happened to be in possession of a cigarette. Of course he wasn't. Most people aren't these days, and I myself no longer smoke—unless, that is, I've been drinking and talking and athletically socializing, and on this particular night I'd been doing plenty of all three. When I asked him if he might find me one, he was dumbfounded. Where, he asked, would he procure such a thing? We were near the stage; the band was between sets. There, I said, pointing straight at the drummer. Now, I didn't know this drummer from Adam, but my hunch turned out to be spot-on. My gallant new acquaintance returned with a handful of American Spirits, and my benefactor gave me a mock salute.

While this story was being told (to some very nice people, including one guy who happens to be a billionaire), I was standing there, not just a little embarrassed, it having dawned on me that I was not looking all that hot in this narrative. Forward, demanding, trashy even, are just a few of the adjectives that come to mind, but my generous new pal offered up the anecdote as proof of my ingenuity and clairvoyant powers instead. Clearly, he doesn't know much about drummers.

Drummers are badasses. I knew if there were anyone who'd still have a pack or two handy, it would be him (chefs remain reliable sources too, of course, but they were way back in the cooking tent). My great friend Bill Dunlap was a drummer in a rock-and-roll group called the Imperial Show Band before he straightened up and became a painter (and now a writer too) instead. The pantheon of jazz and rock-and-roll greats is crowded: Ginger Baker, Roy Haynes, Philly Joe Jones, Charlie Watts, Buddy Rich, Keith Moon, and Questlove, just to name a handful. If you are too young to know who most of these people are, download their music at once. Without Watts, there would be no Rolling Stones. Ditto Baker and Cream. That sound you hear at the end of the Who's "Love, Reign o'er Me"? "Moon the Loon" flipping over his drum set. Also, I am not in the least bit ashamed to say that Ringo was always my favorite Beatle, though admittedly my attachment was not immediate. I was three and a half and in Nashville when the band made their *Ed Sullivan Show* debut. For the life of me, I couldn't figure out why my entire extended family had gathered breathlessly around my Uncle Evans's snowy TV set to watch what I had assumed would be insects crawling across the screen. Once I got it, Ringo was my man.

One of the more extraordinary facts about my extraordinary mother is that when she was a very chaste sophomore at Vanderbilt, she had a sort of thing with a drummer named, I swear, Otto Bash. A date (a presentable one, a fellow her own age) had taken her to hear Otto at the Celtic Room in Nashville's notorious nightclub district Printer's Alley (liquor by the drink, illegal until 1967 in Nashville, was readily available). Fairly quickly, Mama lost interest in the date and took up with Otto, who was almost twice her age. She recalls going to a party at Otto's apartment where "at least twenty half-nude women" mingled and danced. Inexplicably, she brought Otto home to her parents' house in Belle Meade, where she still lived, and that was the end of that. When my grandfather, a former naval officer and still very fit star baseball player, discovered them playing cards in the library, he picked Otto up by the scruff of his neck ("sort of like a cat," my mother says) and escorted him out of the house. "He was a different experience for me, I can tell you." I'll say. But I get it. First of all, there's that name. Second of all, the lure of the minstrel is age-old and powerful.

For example, in the late eighteenth century a Frenchman named Christophe Colomb, who claimed to be a descendant of Christopher Columbus (and who was said to be on the run as a result of a plot involving the French Revolution), turned up on Louisiana's River Road, home to the indigo and sugarcane planters who were then the country's wealthiest men. One of those planters, Marius Bringier, grew fond of the charming Colomb, an itinerant painter, raconteur, and musician. Not wanting to be deprived of his company, Bringier arranged for his daughter

Fanny to marry him, and in 1801 built the couple a stunning Greek Revival box called Bocage that still stands on the banks of the Mississippi. Fanny, all of fourteen at the time, wrote in her diary that she was a tad freaked out about the compelled union, but in no time she too succumbed to the charms of her husband. Fanny ran the plantation while Colomb hung out on his ornamental barge, reclining beneath a hand-painted silk canopy, playing tunes on his guitar. Along the way, the couple managed to have eight children, and by all accounts their marriage was a blissful one.

I was about Fanny's age when I fell for a similarly captivating minstrel, Leonard Cohen. I wore out the grooves of Cohen's *Songs from a Room* on the stereo I took with me to boarding school, and Scotch-taped his dreamy photo (the album sleeve) to the ceiling above my dorm-room bed. The first LP I bought with my own money was Bob Dylan's *Planet Waves*, and let me stop and say right here that his Nobel was long overdue. If you don't believe that lyrics are literature, listen to "Visions of Johanna" or pretty much the entirety of *Blood on the Tracks*, which is not unlike reading Chekhov. If you don't believe he's soulful and sexy as all get-out, even now, listen to Joan Baez singing "Yellow Coat." Or to Dylan's own "Something There Is About You" or "Sara" or "Tonight I'll Be Staying Here with You." I could go on. Anyway, the best songwriters have always been poets. Cohen's endlessly romantic "Alexandra Leaving" was based on C. P. Cavafy's "The God Abandons Antony"—except that, naturally, Alexandria the city becomes Alexandra the woman.

When I was in college, I turned my attention to a musician from my hometown whom I actually knew. As with Otto Bash and my mother, he was at least twice my age, and even though he lived in L.A. and I lived in D.C., we got together whenever we were in the Delta, which was a fair amount. He was heavenly to look at, had a real-live band called Fun with Animals, and when he played the piano he was so emotionally and physically all in, it was impossible to take your eyes off him. During one spring break visit home, I had a dinner party at my parents' house that ended up with everyone taking a dip in the unlit pool, and when we got out, I noticed that the object of my affection was missing—along with my best friend. Almost a whole day later they were found, communing in a cotton field, by the local sheriff, who had been roused by my friend's increasingly frantic mother and rather more disgusted father. I was a tad miffed myself, but I forgave her pretty quick. I knew, after all. At the time, he'd been testing out a ballad that began, "With Jack Daniel's for company, you go wherever you please." The chorus contained the line "But I'll wrap my love around you, all night long," and you sort of had to hear it, but, trust me, it was heartbreaking in all the right ways. Plus, the best friend in question (and yes, she still retains the title) happens to be a musician too. In fairly short order, they ended up getting married and stayed that way long enough to have a son, a talented chef and a fine, funny young man who is one of the people I love the most in this world.

When I thank God for their union, I'm not even being magnanimous. But I knew it wouldn't last—that's not what these guys are for. Which is not to say they can't be useful in other ways when it comes to marriage. On the night my parents gave a holiday party to celebrate my engagement to the man who would have been my first husband, an old flame—a musician and songwriter of prodigious gifts—turned up at midnight, uninvited, at the front door. Without much of a word, he sat down at the piano. My best friend, already single again by then, called down the street for a guitar she knew my neighbor had gotten for Christmas. The would-be groom went to bed, which should have tipped me off right then and there. The rest of us stayed up past dawn singing impromptu songs written, improbably, about the recent fall of the Soviet Union. One began, "Dubček is a redneck"; another, a take on the great blues classic (at least in my hometown) "Greenville's Smokin', Leland's Burnin' Down," referenced (rather starkly) Ceausescu's leg smoking and Bucharest burning down. I'm sorry, but you can't help but be crazy about someone who is that agile with both his brain and his picking fingers, especially at that hour of the morning. When he launched into one of my favorites, a song he wrote containing the line "You make me nervous when you lay down beside me," I realized a particular sort of romance had been missing from my life for a little too long.

The good thing is that these days romance is as easy to call up as tapping the iTunes app (which I did, a lot, in November 2016 during the days after Leonard Cohen's death). Also, even though all my boyfriends are dropping like flies (the loss of Cohen, Leon Russell, and Glenn Frey in a single year meant a serious depletion of my life's sound track singers), those left standing are still, valiantly, hard at it. A few years ago, my parents were in Nashville for an event and my mother got wind of the fact that not only were the Rolling Stones staying in their hotel, they were playing the next night at the Vanderbilt Stadium. Mama bribed the doorman for tickets, and my father, mightily fearful that he would have to attend, decamped. I was happily pressed into duty instead and hopped a plane immediately. It was great: Mick did his indefatigable thing, Keith wore a fetching chiffon leopard print duster, and Charlie was as infallibly cool as ever. Afterward we went to Morton's, split a big piece of rare meat, and toasted our evening with a nice bottle of red. As it happens, Morton's is very near the old Printer's Alley. It was that night that I learned all about Otto Bash.

Hello Mother,
Hello Father

THE SUMMER AFTER MY EIGHTH-GRADE YEAR, THE SON of close family friends—on whom I'd had an enormous crush forever—got married. He wore seersucker suits and played the guitar, and, the year before, when he had told me he would wait for me, I'd believed him. Upon the announcement of the engagement, I locked myself in my room for three days with a scratchy LP of Rachmaninoff's Piano Concerto no. 2 (this was far too serious a business for the Carpenters or even Joni Mitchell, both of whom had hits that year). Still bereft, but by now also thoroughly bored, I hatched a plan. I was going to look so good at his wedding I would make that man sorry.

This proved to be easier for a thirteen-year-old than one might think. I had a summer job at our town's ultrachic department store, Hafter-Blum, fetching coffee and lunch and putting price tags on the frocks. I learned the beauty of a bias cut and the difference between crepe and crepe de chine, and kept an eye out for my wedding showstopper. By late June, when the big day arrived, I'd saved enough of my wages to buy a backless, knife-pleated Cacharel cotton dress with a tiny flower print and a lowish square-cut neckline. I'd heard my mother ordering shoes from Neiman Marcus over the phone so many times I knew the name of her salesman, who sent purchases overnight via the Continental Trailways from Dallas (our early-1970s version of FedEx). He dispatched a pair of creamy snake-skin Charles Jourdans with a three-inch stacked heel I wore well into my twenties. My grandmother, my partner in all things inappropriately sophisticated, sent me diamond earrings and a perfect wide-brimmed straw hat. Needless to say, the groom didn't notice, and my mother was suitably aghast. No matter. I'd learned a powerful lesson in the healing power of glamour, especially when applied to wounded pride.

Alas, mine was a short-lived transformation. The next morning, instead of a glass slipper, I was given a new pair of Keds and a seat on a Blue Bird bus bound for a Baptist Bible camp in Mentone, Alabama. It was a tragic turn of events that had been engineered by my mother a few months earlier when she announced that she and my father had decided I'd become entirely too cynical for my age. This particular camp, she said, was just the answer; it had done wonders for so-and-so. She knew I would love it. Spoiler alert: I did not love it.

It is worth pointing out that the best antidote for cynicism might not be a decidedly unpicturesque place in the piney woods run by two sanctimonious old ladies who banned comic books on Sundays and served food so bad it required lashings of nasty treacle syrup from ever-present pitchers (thus dashing my hopes that at least I would get really, really skinny). Every morning at dawn we were dragged off to a formation of damp and freezing-cold rocks to pray, and every evening in our cabins we were made to say—out loud—all the things we were thankful for. I hate getting up early, I don't like a forced march, and it's nobody's beeswax what I'm thankful for. Plus, I could never think of a thing to say except the fact that I would one day be getting the hell out of there, which I thought wise to keep to myself.

To be fair, my mother had adored camp. She went to Green Cove and Rockbrook, and she was so convinced the sailing skills she'd learned at Camp Nagawicka had stood the test of time, she once rented us a sailboat at a Disney resort, and we had to be towed back to the dock. All the girls I grew up with couldn't wait to head off to Kahdalea and Illahee every summer, and even my cousin Frances, who had good reason to be a cynic, looked forward to her six weeks away. (But then she went to a cool camp, Merrie-Woode, where she got to make an actual gold ring instead of a plastic lanyard, a hideous neckpiece I could never master the art of.) I get that I was the odd girl out, but I didn't find it remotely strange that I preferred hanging out in an air-conditioned store surrounded by beautiful clothes and cool adults rather than a hot cabin with grubby children I didn't know. My dear friend Libby Page loved Green Cove so much that she and her daughter still attend annual reunions where I swear they sing camp songs. I cannot imagine voluntarily listening to "Kumbaya"; camp even put me off pine trees.

Also, by the time I was packed off to Alabama, it wasn't as if I hadn't already had the experience. I'd attended a two-week Girl Scout camp, Cedar Point, in Grenada, Mississippi, for two summers and had gone for a month to a place called Tumbling

Waters somewhere in Georgia. So I knew well that camp was full of stuff that made me profoundly uncomfortable: spiders; bunk beds; cold, dark lakes (I prefer my water clear and moving); sleeping on the ground; bows and arrows; girls en masse. Plus, seriously bad things happened while I was gone. My beloved black-and-white cocker spaniel, Buddy (born a week before I was), got run over in our driveway by the cable man, and my riding teacher sold Mary Poppins, the gentle white pony I'd ridden since I was four.

Despite all that, I thought I'd been a pretty good sport about those initial forays until I read the letters home my mother recently unearthed and sent me in a box. In one, from Cedar Point, I reported that my cabinmates were so lame we'd "made a complete flop" of skit night, and that it was so "unbearably" hot I was bound to have "a heat stroke." Further, I hugely resented having to take "three Girl Scout bites" out of everything including our morning grits, which I despise (unless of course they are mixed with good things like sharp cheddar and jalapeños rather than the camp's cheap margarine). From Tumbling Waters, I wrote that the girls were "mostly Yankees, snobs, and racists," and that the much-touted biscuits "are not even as good as the ones Mama gets at Sunflower." The light in my bottom bunk was so bad I could barely read or write and the tap water so cold it was painful to wash my face. You get the idea—the box is a big one.

Still, there had been a few high points. At Cedar Point, I won a talent show by singing "Raindrops Keep Fallin' on My Head" while wearing a trench coat and holding a red flowered umbrella. This begs the question of why I'd thought to include in my trunk an actual Burberry trench, a gift, naturally, from my grandmother. Also, my fervent desire notwithstanding, I am not, in fact, a very good singer. At Tumbling Waters, I made friends with my very cool counselor, Penny from North Carolina, whom I was later allowed to visit at Stephens College, and the pottery bowl I made in arts and crafts still sits on my father's dresser.

There were no such high points at the Bible camp, just countless moments all but engineered to foster, rather than fight, cynicism. Before a field trip to Six Flags Over Georgia, for example, the ladies called a meeting to declare that since we all came from families of different means, it had been decided that we could take with us no more than $7.35 in spending money, no matter how much we might have stashed in our cabins. How they arrived at that particular number ("in the interest of fairness") still boggles the mind. Also, our means were hardly that diverse since tuition was, even then, up in the thousands. (Note to my parents: You were robbed.) I myself had stashed a hundred bucks under my (very thin) mattress— I'd been a working girl, after all—and I determined to spend every cent of it after this ludicrous decree. I bought popcorn and cotton candy and fudge for pretty much everyone except the super-righteous chicks I knew to be tattlers. I bought my parents tacky key chains, my little brothers T-shirts and toys and hats I had to hide in my clothes. When we returned and were made to pledge ("before God") that we'd abided by the rule, I didn't bat an eye. I knew He'd understand.

In fairly short order I decided to forgive my mother. For one thing, there was a copy of James Taylor's brand-new *Walking Man* LP on my bed when I got home, and the subject of camp was never, ever, brought up again. Also, what I think she finally figured out is that I was never really much of a cynic, just a fairly observant kid healthily attuned to the foibles of human nature. At heart, I've always been a romantic. It's just that to this day I find very little romance in shower shoes, outdoor latrines, and 6:00 A.M. wake-up bells. Fortunately, I had visions of strappy sandals and a swirling, knife-pleated skirt to see me through. The dress still hangs in my closet.

A Moving Experience

"IF YOU WANT THIS, YOU BETTER COME GET IT. NOW."
That was my mother, yelling down the phone pretty much
every week beginning in October 2016, when she announced
that she was selling our family house, until May 2017, when
she and my father moved into a nearby new one. The items in
question ranged from my childhood country mouse house and
the riding boots I'd last worn in the ninth grade to a winged
chair and a crusty trumeau mirror I'd always wished was mine.
Whatever she didn't want, she wanted gone, immediately.

She was on a mission, an urgent one that none of us had
seen coming, though there had been a few hints. There was, for
example, the catfish fry she and my father so graciously hosted
each year during the Delta Hot Tamale Festival to thank the
many chefs and writers and artists who come to contribute to
the improvement of our town. "This is the last one," she'd said
as she directed the hanging of lanterns from the branches of

the live oak tree spreading over our back terrace and draped cloths over the round tables that dotted the lawn from the terrace to the pool. I'd thought she'd simply tired of the annual effort, but less than a week later she broke the news: "I've found a house, and we're selling this one." I was stunned. "This one" was the house we'd moved into when I was two and my brothers were not yet born. It was the house my mother had made so eminently magical and welcoming with endless additions that drove my father mad. ("Remind me what it was that you liked about this house in the first place," he would say as each new project started.) It was the house surrounded by trees and gardens she'd lovingly created as a novice: a young woman, barely twenty-one, who'd left the well-manicured environs of Belle Meade in Nashville to marry my father and create a life in the comparative wilds of the Mississippi Delta.

My mother had grown up on the banks of Richland Creek, a civilized rivulet filled with moss and watercress and rocks on which she and her cousin sunned themselves. Our house, on the other hand, was on land that had once been part of Rattlesnake Bayou Plantation, named after the muddy stream that once provided water for the whole town—as well as the rattlesnakes that never exactly cleared out of our yard. The property had been divided into spacious lots in the 1930s, when our house was built next door to the "developer," Mr. Smith, who lived in an expanded version of the original plantation kitchen and who still kept horses and cows and a bull that once got loose and landed in our swimming pool. A levee, built by slaves in the 1830s as the only protection against the ravages of the Mississippi, still fronted our house and three more. On the rare occasions that snow fell, we sledded down its banks; in spring it was covered with the tiny heirloom daffodils with the heavenly scent my mother brought from Tennessee. The previous owners had pretty much left our six acres as it was, with clumps of cypress in the low-lying land in front of the levee and ancient pecans dotting the lawn. Mama got to work immediately, planting more cypress, dozens of magnolias, pin oaks and live oaks, crape myrtles and hollies. She planted borders in the back and thousands of bulbs in the front: more daffodils, crocuses, tulips, and snowdrops. There were masses of swamp iris to greet arrivals at the beginning of our long gravel drive; the summer border was a riot of hydrangeas and lilies and Queen Anne's lace.

I loved that yard. I used it as my own private theater, wandering about while acting out dramas in which I imagined myself to look like Anna Maria Alberghetti (an actress I'd seen on *The Mike Douglas Show*), playing a singer who faced her many tribulations stoically while belting out the songs I'd learned in school ("If I Had a Hammer," "Michael, Row the Boat Ashore"), terrifying the squirrels with a voice that is, in real life, not so hot. I read for hours lying on my stomach, picked wildflowers and made clover chains, created "houses" of my own inside the hollows of the vast honeysuckle hedges. A fenced-off area contained the pear tree that was my favorite roost, a fig orchard, and the mostly unmarked graves of: seven dogs; untold numbers of goldfish, turtles, gerbils, and guinea pigs; and my beloved gray cat West Virginia, named after what was, perversely, my favorite state at age three. There was also the ruin of the pen that housed the pet ducks we finally let loose in the lake and my beloved rabbit Carrots, whom Mr. Smith's dastardly dalmatians made such a feast of that all that was left to bury was his fur.

My father had complained about the yard and its massive upkeep off and on for years, but I know he never dreamed he'd actually be pried from his lair. We're sentimentalists, he and I, and anyway, what would we do about his books and all the stuff crammed into every drawer and every closet, not to mention all the memories? But as much as I loved every moment I spent in that house—the joyful, the profoundly sad, and all the ones in between—I was surprised to realize that I admired my mother's resolve even more. At eighty, she was not heading to a retirement community but embarking on a new adventure and a fresh project (naturally, the house they bought required a ton of tinkering and, yep, an addition). The purge the move engendered was not just a lightening of the load (the house had become such a repository I'm surprised its foundation had not sunk deep into the fabled Mississippi mud), but also an exhilarating lightening of the spirit (my mother's). I, on the other hand, was the beneficiary not just of my childhood possessions and the odd piece of furniture, but of massive boxes containing every photo ever taken with me in it and every letter I ever wrote home.

Then there were the dozens of champagne flutes, water goblets, sherbet cups (sherbet cups!), wineglasses, and one of the three sets of breakfast china (breakfast china!) Mama was given when she got married. I toted out felt bag after felt bag of silver trays and soufflé dishes, boxes of embroidered place mats, and the stemmed garnet glasses that were only ever hauled out at Christmas. Clearly it's time for me to write another book on entertaining, but what to do with my Woodmen of the World history award plaque from eighth grade or, indeed, the mouse house?

Meanwhile, my parents' new place is beautiful and light filled and stocked only with the treasures that mean the most to both of them. When I visited the old house just before it sold, it was shockingly empty, but the memories had not yet left. In the quiet, I heard the ghosts of countless parties past: the tinkling of laughter and the lilting female voices I can still identify drifting from the pool house to my bedroom window on late summer evenings; William F. Buckley, Jr., banging out "Cielito Lindo" on our piano accompanied by a close friend who invariably arrived with his vibraphone; the pop and fizz of the Roman candles my friends and I were allowed to set off on the front lawn every Christmas night while the adults carried on inside. There were birthday parties featuring the full-size merry-go-round that was a gift from my extravagant grandmother, legendary teenage summer bashes held when my parents were out of town that required heavy cash and comic book payoffs to my brothers, who were charged with retrieving the hundreds of Budweiser pop-tops off the bottom of the pool. There was my fortieth birthday dance, a fabulous wedding that kicked off a pretty good run of a marriage, endless cookouts, and the aforementioned catfish fries.

There were sad times too, of course. When my paternal grandparents were killed in a car wreck about two hours out of town, my parents took off to the scene and by the time they got back, at least a hundred cars lined the driveway. My grandfather's contemporaries were sitting stone-faced and stiff-backed on the sofas, toddies between their legs, while ladies from the church had positioned themselves by the front and back doors with spiral notebooks in which to write down who had brought the various casseroles and cakes that had already begun to arrive. When the funeral was finally held, on a rainy Easter Sunday afternoon, we had already hosted a nonstop three-day wake. Still, my mother laid out more food for those who remained and lit a fire, a spark from which set our shake roof ablaze. After a valiant effort by one of my cousins, the fire department arrived to stanch the flames, followed by my father's best friend and business partner, Barthell Joseph, who drove across the front yard and bounded up the porch steps, wild-eyed and demanding to see that "Tyrone" (his nickname for my father) remained alive and well.

It is those memories that remind me that it's not the house that held us all, but the larger community, which remains in one way or another still intact. My parents' new house is just down the street from Barthell's widow. I'm building my own house, a tiny one, on the narrow lot behind our old house, between a tall fence and the dirt road across from the pasture where I once kept my horse Hi Joe. My closest neighbors will be my childhood friends Amanda and Carl Cottingham— Amanda's father drove us to school in his Mustang convertible every day of my life until Amanda was old enough to drive us herself.

Before the lovely new owners closed on the old house, I'd vowed to host an enormous farewell on the grounds, but then it seemed somehow unnecessary, wrongheaded even. That trusty, sprawling board-and-batten structure had served its purpose and given us plenty. Instead, I decided to take a leaf from Mama's book and look forward. Better by far to host a ground-breaking shindig on my own property or start a new Christmas party tradition at my parents' place. In one of my many boxes there are probably some ancient Roman candles, and I can always bring the garnet glasses.

Part Two

Critters

The Awesome Opossum

LAST SUMMER I HAD THE PLEASURE OF SIGNING BOOKS at Asheville, North Carolina's terrific independent bookstore Malaprop's, which also stocks a variety of very cool postcards. I was struck by one in particular: a delightfully naive pencil drawing of a sweet mama possum toting a passel of babies on her back (*passel* is the correct term for a group of possums, by the way, as in a wake of buzzards or a gaze of raccoons). The drawing was inside an outline of the state of North Carolina, which had, according to the text, designated the Virginia opossum as its state marsupial in 2013.

Without delving too deep into potentially divisive territory here, I would venture that voting for an official marsupial might be a less, um, disruptive use of the North Carolina legislature's time than some of the other stuff they've gotten up to of late. And, you know, it wasn't that hard to choose: *Didelphis virginiana* happens to be the *only* marsupial (pouched mammal) in all of America, and Canada too.

Though there are several species of marsupials called possums in Australia and New Guinea, scientists now believe that all marsupials (including the ancestors of the kangaroo and the koala) originated in North America and that they did so at least sixty-five million years ago. Nobody named them until 1608, when Captain John Smith came up with "opassom," from the Algonquian term meaning "white animal." Folks started dropping the *o* pretty early on, but Smith stuck with it, writing: "An Opassom hath an head like a Swine, and a taile like a Rat, and is of the bignesse of a Cat. Under her belly shee hath a bagge, wherein shee lodgeth, carrieth, and suckleth her young."

The good captain made no note of his sentiments toward the creature, but I could tell that the artist who drew the postcard, Julie Wade, is as crazy about possums as I am. For one thing, she drew hearts in all four corners. It turns out that there's a growing number of folks who also feel fondly toward the much-maligned mammal. Rick Ostfeld, senior scientist at the Cary Institute of Ecosystem Studies in Millbrook, New York, calls possums "the unsung heroes in the Lyme disease epidemic." Unlike the lazier tick carriers Ostfeld studied, including rodents and birds, they are star groomers, he says, "hoovering up more than 95 percent of the ticks that try to feed on them." A single possum can kill a whopping four thousand ticks a week, and they also get rid of a whole bunch of other stuff that most folks would rather not have around. They eat garden pests such as snails and slugs and beetles, they keep roaches and rats at bay by competing for their food or simply killing them when they trespass on their territory, and, thanks to their remarkably efficient immune systems, they can consume rattlesnakes and cottonmouths without being affected by their venom. Further, unlike the great majority of other mammals, they are happy to dine on carrion, a proclivity that has earned them the sobriquet "sanitation workers of the wild."

They are also possessed of an impressive set of physical attributes, not least of which is a forked penis, a curiosity that led colonial Americans (who apparently conducted some mighty close anatomical inspections) to believe that the male possum bred with the female through her nostrils. They do not, in fact, hang from their prehensile tails (or at least not for long—once they're grown they're way too heavy); they use them instead for stability while climbing and to carry bundles of grasses for their nests. Like some primates, they have opposable "thumbs" on their hind feet, which make them uncommonly agile, and they have more teeth—fifty—than any other mammal except the killer whale and the giant armadillo. The latter gave rise to the expression "grinning like a possum eating a sweet potato"—or a persimmon, which they especially like, but you can fill in the blank with almost anything. A friend of mine swears that when he kicked a mule to see if it was really dead, two possums emerged from its rear end, an admittedly disgusting image that might well explain the origin of another adjective having to do with a grin, but hey, this is nature, after all.

A possum is a nocturnal, naturally gentle sort who tries admirably hard to keep to him- or herself, so all those teeth are rarely put to use biting humans. "Playing possum" is a real thing—an involuntary response to danger in which the creatures fall into a catatonic state for up to four hours—as well as a trait I'd most love to have. Imagine being able to go rigid and stare off into space every time someone bugged or bored you (this is sometimes preceded by belching and hissing, which would also be pretty damn effective). The late columnist Robert Novak once hit the floor of my living room after being treated to a lengthy monologue by the pedantic tax reformist Grover Norquist. An ambulance was duly summoned, but by the time it arrived, Novak was fine and I knew exactly what had happened, having talked to Norquist myself. One does what one can to survive.

The downside for possums is that these instincts are often switched on in the middle of a highway, where they spend a lot of time munching on roadkill, making the automobile the species' most effective predator. Though said to be smarter than dogs, they are slow to get out of the way, a state of affairs that leads to the rather succinct lyrics of a ten-minute Phish song: ". . . riding down the road one day and someone hit a possum . . . The road was his end, His end was the road . . . Whoa possum, possum, your end is the road."

For a long time, the possum's end was also the serving platter. The marsupials were introduced in the western United States primarily as a food source, and as late as the 1960s, *Joy of Cooking* included them along with directions for proper scraping and cooking. Even now, on a website run by "Recipe Girl," there is a plethora of possum recipes, including one for "Sweet Taters and Possum" that begins, without irony: "First catch a young fat possum. This in itself affords excellent sport on moonlit nights in the fall." The nation's twenty-seventh president, William Howard Taft, was so fond of possums that folks started sending them to the White House in the mail, a practice that caused a bit of a brouhaha when some Leesville, Louisiana, hunters left a live possum addressed to Taft in the post office's package department and the traumatized animal chewed up the rest of the mail in the box.

It all started in January 1909 when the president-elect asked that possum be served at a banquet given by the Atlanta Chamber of Commerce in his honor. The natives of Worth County formed a Possum Committee in order to hunt and provide "one hundred fat possums," which were then boiled, baked, and basted with a newly invented "special sauce." Sweet potatoes were served as an accompaniment, and since "liquid from foreign vineyards" was illegal in Georgia, "a lady admirer" of Taft's brewed a barrel of persimmon beer for the occasion. Taft was said to have gobbled up his personal possum so fast that a nearby doctor advised him to slow down. But he kept up the pace throughout his one-term presidency, driving up the cost of possum from one dollar to ten dollars per carcass and serving up a twenty-six-pound possum at his first White House Thanksgiving. Thus began a drive to entice the president into putting other such regional delicacies on the culinary map. In Wyoming he was served prairie dog, and when it was discovered that the people of Louisiana planned to serve him alligator on a visit to the state, the *New York Times* was moved to publish an admonishing editorial: "It is no part of the president's duty to eat strange foods merely to satisfy neighborhood pride. We earnestly beg Mr. Taft to stop with the 'possum."

Waxing philosophical, a member of the Possum Committee told the *Worth County Local* that "a possum is not like anything else under the sun, except another possum." While this is certainly true, there are people who bear at least a passing resemblance. His close-set eyes and distinctive nose earned George Jones the nickname the Possum long before he was saddled with the less affectionate No Show. Ezra Pound called T. S. Eliot Old Possum, and it must be said that Eliot's nose was his most prominent feature. It's ironic, then, that the world's most famous possum, Walt Kelly's Pogo, didn't look all that much like one, though he possessed many of the creature's more noble attributes, including a certain equanimity, humility, and the good sense to avoid trouble.

Indeed, Pogo was possum as everyman, and some of the happiest hours of my childhood were spent on my father's lap while he read the comic strip aloud to me, hee-hee-heeing throughout. One of Daddy's many fine qualities is his endless ability to laugh at himself, as well as at the general ridiculousness of his fellow man, a particularly useful trait if you happen to live where we live. Pogo's full name was Ponce de Leon Montgomery County Alabama Georgia Beauregard Possum, a not-so-subtle send-up of the aristocratic airs of a certain breed of Southerner. But Pogo himself was as literally down to earth as the other members of his species.

When he and his cohorts embark on an expedition beyond the confines of home, the Okefenokee Swamp, he sends back a message: "We have met the enemy and he is us." Yep, it surely is, but Pogo remains ever hopeful. When he tells Porky Pine that he reckons "ev'ry critter's heart is in the right place," Porky answers, "If you gotta be wrong 'bout somethin', that's 'bout the best thing to be wrong 'bout." There is plenty more wisdom for our always unsettled times, including, also from Porky, "Don't take life so serious, son. It ain't nohow permanent." It's good stuff not just for our age (though, man, it would be fun to have Kelly around about now) but for the ages—let's not forget that Kelly began writing the strip in 1943 and among the politicians he lampooned were Senator Joe McCarthy (Simple J. Malarkey) and Vice President Spiro Agnew (a hyena who spoke in alliterative nonsense). At any rate, it's instructive to look back at the vast cache of strips. You never know: It could well be the unassuming possum who leads us out of our own collective swamp.

Alternatively, you could just drink yourself into oblivion with a cocktail named the Possum Drop, a creation of the legendary Snake and Jake's Christmas Club Lounge, a pluperfect New Orleans dive lit solely by Christmas-tree lights and guarded by a dog named Odysseia. One night a possum fell through a ceiling tile and landed on a customer, and the drink, a shot of Jägermeister dropped into a pint of Schlitz, was born. Snake and Jake's is not unlike Pogo's Okefenokee: slightly dangerous, filled with characters, and completely cut off from the outside world. I bet even the possum wanted to stick around.

Big Racks and Perfect Parties

SOME TIME AGO IN NEW ORLEANS, I WAS AT A BENEFIT for historic houses when my dinner partner, a tiny bit bored with the proceedings at hand, started telling me all about a weekend he'd spent at a nearby farm. The room was loud and there was an auction going on, so when I heard him say something about deer and fences, I remarked as to how his host's fence must be a hell of a thing in order to keep all those pesky deer out.

I'd just seen an episode from the first season of the TV show, *Homeland*, the one in which returning Marine/is-he-or-isn't-he terrorist Damian Lewis takes his government-issue rifle and blows away a deer in his suburban D.C. backyard. The deer had made the mistake of munching on his wife's flower beds—twice—and Lewis's character is a tad on the jittery side. So I was thinking about that scene and how the deer might have made it if only those beds had been fenced in (which in turn led to a mini-reverie about an even more riveting episode in which Lewis and

Claire Danes's bipolar CIA agent have one of the most intense love scenes ever on TV or, for that matter, in the movies) when my companion brought me back to the reality of the ballroom: "No, no," he said. "The fence is to keep the deer from getting out."

Out? Oh yes, he said, the deer are specially bred does and bucks that originate from Texas, and they get a nice rich high-protein diet and wander around in a very pretty place surrounded by very tall fences. So now I was convinced that I really must be hearing wrong, because while I get the point of breeding, say, chickens, and I'm a big fan of a free-range bird's superior meat, deer already range so freely that at least 1.5 million of them get hit by cars every year. A particularly memorable front-page photograph in my Mississippi hometown's newspaper a few years back featured a buck jumping through the plate-glass window of the local travel agency—the spring floods had driven a veritable herd of them in search of high ground, where they ranged right on up Main Street. I couldn't imagine who in the world would think it necessary to—on purpose—breed any more of them and I said so.

When he responded with "It's a guy thing," I finally understood that the "farm" he visited does not have a thing to do with the quality of the venison or even how picturesque the whitetails happen to be. (I have a very rich acquaintance who once imported some extremely expensive and especially attractive European cows to her weekend place in Connecticut for the simple reason that they decorated the view.) It's about the same thing guys have been hunting for—on pretty much every front—since time began: bigger and better racks.

At this point I was curious (and rude) enough to pull my

iPhone from my evening bag. A quick search of "deer breeding" revealed that I was way behind the curve on the subject.
In Texas alone the deer breeding business brings in almost
$3 million a year. The first breeding operation that popped up,
DeerStar, advertises "genetically improved" UltraDoes that are
artificially inseminated with the semen from bucks with names
like Gladiator's Hammer and Ultimate Weapon, to produce the
white-tailed version of Arnold Schwarzenegger back when he
was all bulked up (and, by his own admission, on steroids), only
with way bigger headgear.

Their progeny and thousands of others just like them are
raised in pens (the babies get bottles, the adults probiotics) and
then released on high-fenced ranches just before hunting season. Super Trophy Class bucks, usually created with semen
from Northern deer that outweigh the local whitetails, have
multipointed antlers that score as high as three hundred
inches—so big and bizarrely shaped that one disapproving outdoor columnist compared them to "mangrove swamps." But he
seems to be in the minority. At 4M Ranch, for example, the
"philosophy" is "simple": "Size Does Matter! Remember, if you
want Big Whitetails, you must breed BIG ON BIG!"

The point of all this of course is that size sells. Hunters have
been known to pay $10,000 (and in some cases an astonishing
$100,000) to bag a super buck. Which is where the fences
come in. You don't want your potential gold mine to actually
have a shot at getting away. Plus, when a buck is in possession
of semen worth anywhere from $3,000 to $35,000 a pop, you
can't have him spreading it around just anywhere. On websites
like DeerStar's, bloodlines are traced further back than those
of most racehorses. Cloning is not unheard of.

DeerStar, whose motto is "Not just state of the art, the state of nature," seems unaware of how much it is tampering with the latter. The owners claim instead to "have thought many things out in detail to make sure that what we do honors our creator," which is the part where I always get nervous. It rarely ends well when a commercial enterprise (or a political candidate or Pat Robertson—whoever) claims to have an inside track on the wishes of our Lord. Also, I'm not at all sure how He might come down on the subject of dosing up "breeder does" with the sperm of genetically manipulated bucks who have names better suited to professional wrestlers and then charging people a bunch of money to take aim at their offspring. Still, folks persist. One embattled member of the industry told the Texas Deer Association, "Because I'm a deer breeder, sometimes I feel like I'm a Christian at an atheist rally."

I should interject here that I am grateful for my many deer-hunting friends who manage to bag plenty of bucks the old-fashioned way. I make a mean venison chili and I am crazy for a deer head—in fact, I'm a huge fan of taxidermy in general. As I type, the mounted head of a wild boar is shedding all over my office mantel, upon which two stuffed birds from the great Paris taxidermy shop Deyrolle sit. Last year for Christmas, my thoughtful former assistant Bebe Howorth gave me a "basket" made from the body and tail of an armadillo, and one of my greatest regrets is that in a fit of pique at a particularly onerous ex-boyfriend, I got rid of the magnificent stag horns that were the only nice things he'd ever given me.

After I canceled a wedding (different boyfriend, a lot less onerous), my best friend Jessica and I decided to have a black-tie ball for all the people disappointed that they were no longer invited to the Mississippi Delta for the nuptials. The location was a falling-down antebellum mansion once owned by the family of Shelby Foote, and the theme was taxidermy. If you live in the right place, this is an extraordinarily inexpensive way to decorate for a party. All it took was a pickup and two Suburbans we filled with various trophies collected from friends and acquaintances, including a beaver munching on a log, an albino squirrel, and at least a half dozen raccoons and foxes. By the time we'd completed the twenty-mile drive from town to the party site, we'd gained a sizable—and very noisy—canine escort who'd followed us the whole way down the highway.

We suspended geese and ducks from the ballroom ceiling with fishing line and stuffed a bouquet of wildflowers into the mouth of a loggerhead turtle that doubled as a coffee table. A coiled rattlesnake presided over the bar, a panther pounced on the mantel, and a hornet's nest hung from the chandelier above the moss-covered dining room table. Among our own superstars was an entire stuffed deer that greeted guests just outside the front door, and a chair made of the legs, horn, and hide of an elk Jessica's father had gone all the way to Gunnison, Colorado, to kill. (The chair had been his gift to the local Elks Lodge, whose members were vocally unhappy when we came to borrow it for the night—not because they were going to miss the chair, but because it required Bonnie the bartender to leave her post for less than five minutes while she held the door open for us, but I digress.)

Anyway, we also had a band with a height-challenged Cajun washboard player who did backflips across the stage and a brunch the next day on the banks of the Mississippi where Jessica's sister Eden played the piano, and it remains one of the best parties either of us has ever given. The whole thing would have come off without a single hitch had we remembered to put the deer back inside the door before we left.

The deer belonged to the owner of a pawnshop who didn't want to part with his handsome specimen, so it was for sale for what we thought then was the inflated price of something like five hundred or maybe even a thousand dollars. During the night, a dog had its way with the deer's back leg, but we managed to locate an emergency taxidermist to repair the damage. Now I can't believe we didn't just buy the deer in the first place because I would give anything in the world—except, I hasten to add, anywhere between $10,000 and $100,000—to own him. Like every other white-tailed deer I've ever seen, he was very beautiful, but we had no idea how lucky we were that the dog had not chewed on someone's UltraBuck. Perhaps I should take a moment to thank our Creator.

God, Gators, and Gumbo

IN FEBRUARY 2013, JUST BEFORE THE START OF LENT, JIM Piculas, a tour guide at the Insta-Gator Ranch & Hatchery in Covington, Louisiana, posted a letter on his employer's Facebook page from the Most Reverend Gregory M. Aymond, archbishop of New Orleans. Piculas had written Aymond to ask if the Church might classify alligator as a fish, thereby making it okay to eat on the Fridays leading up to Easter. The archbishop wrote back that alligator is indeed "considered in the fish family," and when the response went viral, he took to the local airwaves to confirm his position, which, he added, had been backed by the United States Conference of Catholic Bishops. Piculas did not post his own letter, but judging from Aymond's reply, it was fulsome in its praise of the gator. "I agree with you," Aymond wrote. "God has created a magnificent creature that is important to the state of Louisiana and it is considered seafood." The letter was signed "Sincerely in Christ"—who, it should be noted, did not feed the five thousand with loaves and gators. But I digress.

I am a Presbyterian and a fairly lenient Lenten observer, which means that I rarely get around to giving up anything at all, though in terms of Fridays and food I wouldn't have to suffer much. In addition to okaying gator meat, the bishops agree that the Friday rule does not "technically" forbid "meat juices and liquid foods made from meat . . . meat gravies or sauces, as well as other seasonings or condiments made from animal fat." By that measure it's okay to use beef or chicken stock in your seafood gumbo—or indeed alligator stew—and the Bloody Mary at New Orleans' Cochon, which is enriched with pork stock, would also be perfectly acceptable.

Now, some people might say that these are the kinds of loopholes and elastic definitions that have landed the Church in a spot of trouble of late, but given my own shaky status, I will skip over all that and point out that elastic definitions are sort of a Louisiana thing in general and not limited to the Church, as evidenced by the fact that the state was the last to outlaw cockfighting, in 2008. For decades, the New Orleans newspaper, animal rights activists, and various other folks who held the welfare of the chicken close to their hearts had lobbied hard for a ban. They came close to victory at one point in the 1980s when a cruelty-to-animals law was discovered on the books, but then the state attorney general wrote an opinion saying that chickens were not in fact animals, they were "fowl," and the legislature passed another law to that effect, which meant that the noble cocks could keep on fighting for another two decades.

When they were legal, I attended more than one standing-room-only cockfight, so I was aware of their popularity. But apparently I missed the fact that the appetite for gator in Louisiana is so insatiable that to give it up on one day of the week during a season that lasts little more than a month would be a terrible hardship. At Insta-Gator, where you can also arrange a child's birthday party or purchase "quality alligator products" in the gift shop, the girl on the phone told me they sell "thousands upon thousands" of pounds of gator meat each year. The tail meat sells for a beefy ten dollars per pound, a price driven up by the enormous popularity of the reality show *Swamp People*, as well as an aggressive campaign by the Louisiana Seafood Promotion & Marketing Board, which wholeheartedly agrees with Aymond that gator is within their purview and is positively breathless in its description of the meat's "thrilling" versatility and various other qualities that "make any meal more memorable."

In New Orleans, memorable gator meals can be had at Jacques-Imo's, which has long served an alligator cheesecake, the Parkway Bakery & Tavern, which sells an alligator sausage po'boy, and at Cochon, where it comes fried, accompanied by a chile aioli so good it would enhance (or mask) pretty much anything. Co-owner Donald Link says the main reason he and chef Stephen Stryjewski offer gator on the menu is that they feel an obligation to buy the meat from farmers who are really raising the gators for the far more profitable hide. When I ask Link if he actually likes gator, he says the same thing people invariably say about rattlesnake and all the other disgusting things that I honestly do not believe that the Lord meant us to eat on Fridays or any other day: "It tastes like chicken."

Which leads me back to Aymond's letter and the all-important duck test. You know the one: If it looks like a duck, quacks like a duck . . . then it probably is a duck. It seems to me that a corollary to that test is that if something tastes like chicken, it might ought to be considered meat, or at least something firmly not "in the fish family." You could also make the same case based on the fact that gators do not just taste like chicken, they consume it. There is, for example, the memorable scene in *Live and Let Die* in which the gators' appetite for Roger Moore is whetted by an appetizer of raw poultry parts. Just recently, I met a delightful Brit named Peter Pleydell-Bouverie, who had, in his youth, spent a summer at a ranch outside of Houston, where one of the chief forms of entertainment was feeding fried chicken by the bucketful to an alligator on the premises named Gladys. Despite having landed in a slew of clichés on his maiden trip, he still loves the South and visits often, though he does not eat alligator.

Who can blame him, since gators also have been known to eat deer, panther, black bear, the occasional human, and one another? Under duress they are not above going after an inanimate object, such as the trolling motor of my friend Howard Brent's boat, which was bitten off by a gator during a hunt at Howard's farm, Panther Tract. Panther Tract is located on a gorgeous stretch of swampy wilderness in Yazoo County, Mississippi, not far from where the state's record gator, which weighed in at 697.5 pounds, was killed a week or so prior to Howard's hunt. Due to the ample amount of water on his property, Howard is granted five permits a season by the Mississippi Department of Wildlife, Fisheries, and Parks, which means he can kill ten gators, an already daunting process the department does not make any simpler.

After spotting a gator's eyes in the water, you use a rod and reel to land a grappling hook in his hide, and then you get close enough to immobilize him (sort of) with a snare, a device Howard describes as a noose on a pole akin to what old-fashioned dogcatchers used. The aim, since alligators possess between seventy-four and eighty teeth, is to "try and get that noose tightened up around his mouth, so he won't bite"—the one that attacked the motor was caught by the tail. Only after the gator has been snared is the hunter allowed to take his weapon out of its case, and even then, it's not much of one. "You can't use a rifle or a pistol," says Howard, just a shotgun loaded with bird shot. Further, according to the instructions on the department's website, the hunter must "keep gentle pressure" on the restraining line to keep the gator's head and neck above the surface of the water before placing the shotgun a maximum of six to eight inches from him, aiming for the center of the neck.

Needless to say, it's a process a whole lot easier said than done, especially after a few hours on the water in the pitch-black dark during which time I would bet some alcohol is consumed. "You got to find that little old soft spot behind his head, and it's only about the size of a fifty-cent piece," Howard says. "And then he's moving around the whole time." An average hunt will last from about six in the evening until two or three in the morning, after which the skinning begins and then everyone sits down to a big breakfast. Howard loves the sport of it, but he says they'll eat the meat too, usually fried in an egg batter, but first, he cautions, "you got to hammer the hell out of it to tenderize it." I imagine so. "And what does it taste like?" Oh, you know, he answers back, "Sort of like chicken."

Slugging It Out

As a child, I really loved escargot. The dish (which takes the French—and much sexier—name for "edible land snail") was part of the education in sophisticated dining I received by tagging along with my father on numerous trips to our nation's capital. There was smoked salmon carved tableside and a proper Caesar salad likewise tossed at the old lobby-level restaurant of the Hay-Adams Hotel, where we always stayed. Most exciting, a block or so from the White House, there was escargot and steak frites at the original D.C. "power lunch" spot, Sans Souci.

We dined in the now demolished restaurant so often I became a whiz with the tongs and two-tined fork required to extract the snail from its shell. And the thing itself, drenched in garlicky, herby butter (which was at least half the point, after all), was a chewy pleasure that carried over well into adulthood. Further, the snail happens to be the mascot of my alma mater, the Madeira School. Our motto is *Festina lente* ("Make haste slowly") and the school cheer is "Go, Go, Escargots!" Snails and me were clearly meant to be.

Or at least that was the case until the early 1990s, when I moved into a place in the French Quarter and presided over a magical garden spread out over two courtyards. Snails are no longer my friends. And the thought of actually eating one is—pardon the (sort of) pun—completely off the table.

The tide began to turn early in my Bourbon Street tenure when I was awakened—at three in the morning—by the repeated sound of metal hitting brick. Terrified, I crept out onto the balcony and saw my landlady crouched over a bunch of slugs and snails she'd swept into a pile, wielding a huge machete. I thought she'd gone mad, but then I began to invest—heavily—in the garden and was driven to a similar point. The space was the perfect brown snail breeding ground. Walled on all sides, it was essentially a giant terrarium, full of the moisture the snails crave and possessed of endless spots for them to hide from the relentless daytime sun. It turned out that my landlady was not at all nuts (at least on this one subject); nighttime is the best time to catch them, and hacking them to bits is pretty much the only effective way to get rid of them.

The snails glided all over the place (and not all that damn slowly from the looks of things) on a muscular foot, leaving disgusting trails of slime and lacy holes in almost every herbaceous plant and all of my citrus. I tried bowls of beer and sprinkled the recommended coffee grounds and eggshells in the dirt to no avail. I bought hundreds of pounds of snail bait only to find their mucus all over the pellets, which never once impeded their targets. According to the website veggiegardener.com,

"Crushing is the most common method of destruction." Yep. But instead of a machete, I resorted to bricks, old shoes, a rusty shovel. And that's the thing: Once you see a nasty pile of crushed snails in all their viscous glory, you figure out that the sauce you once enjoyed on similar mollusks would taste better on anything but. Then I read that the first step in preparing them as food is to purge them of "the likely undesirable contents of their digestive systems." Case closed.

Even without the snails, gardening in New Orleans is not for the faint of heart. On Bourbon Street I had a monumental stand of banana trees that came with their own set of problems (such is the stickiness of their sap, you need a virtual hazmat suit to trim them). When I moved to First Street, I planted a large live oak instead. It was beautiful, it grew like mad, its lovely curvy limbs shaded an equally lovely dining pergola. Which became a problem when I learned that buck moth caterpillars love oak trees as much as snails loved my courtyards. Covered in hollow spines attached to a poisonous sac, the caterpillars fell off the tree by the hundreds, creating a carpet of furry black land mines. This is not conducive to pleasant dining, nor is it conducive to a happy dog. Henry the beagle stepped on so many that in a single (mercifully short) season, he'd have to get as many as a half dozen cortisone shots.

There is a remedy for them, of course. And like most things in my former First Street garden, it required a hefty check to my trusty tree man, John Benton. I first interviewed Benton, the proprietor of Bayou Tree, for a story I wrote after a swarm of flying Formosan termites ate an entire beam of the Bourbon Street house in a single evening. When we put in the garden of the new house, he was my first call. Little did I know that he and his guys would also be the property's most frequent visitors.

For one thing, even without the walls on all sides, the terrarium effect remained in full force. During the eight years we lived on First, I think there may have been one semi-hard freeze. The long "wall" of hollies I put in to screen my irritating neighbor's house grew at such a rate we trimmed at least ten feet off the top every year. I spent whole weekends hacking ginger and trimming the seemingly endless tendrils of Confederate jasmine and fig vine. The upside was that the brand-new garden, designed by the brilliant Ben Page and divided into five "rooms," looked as though it had been there forever. And Benton and I, by necessity, became fast friends. I advised him on affairs of the heart, recommended books, raged when he put the wrong grass in, adored him when he rid us of the caterpillars. Still, no matter how lush it looked as a whole, individual plants, like people, have minds of their own. On a field trip across Lake Pontchartrain, I bought a stunning variety of gardenias that made a fragrant hedge beneath the double parlor windows. Loaded with blossoms, the bushes grew so fast that Benton asked, "What have you been feeding those things? Chickens?" We laughed and marveled and laughed again. And then, not long afterward, they died. Every single one of them, for no apparent reason. We replaced them with cloudlike drifts of pittosporum, which ended up looking even more beautiful. Still, I was hurt. If gardens require courage, they also demand a thick skin.

Which leads me to the squirrels. Now, my mother has been in the gardening business a lot longer than I. Our former Mississippi Delta yard was not much more than a field when we moved in more than fifty years ago, and now it most closely resembles a wildlife preserve. The last time I visited before the house was sold, Baltimore orioles were stealing the nectar from dozens of hummingbird feeders. Two families of foxes made homes beneath various stands of magnolias. But the one form of wildlife my mother cannot abide is squirrels: They ate the feed of her beloved birds and chewed on the eaves of our house. She once persuaded Harvey Tackett, the late sheriff of Washington County, to send a half dozen deputies from his department to shoot them from our trees. I was aghast. My childhood copy of *The Tale of Squirrel Nutkin* is still stashed in my nightgown drawer, and I have always adored Dürer's *Two Squirrels, One Eating a Hazelnut*, a print of which adorned my first cousin's bedroom. When I was a young visitor at the aforementioned Hay-Adams, the angelic Filipino barman gave me bowls of peanuts to feed to the mostly gray squirrels in Lafayette Park. (This was a far kinder, gentler era, when it was safe for ten-year-olds to visit the park under the distant supervision of a hotel doorman and well before threats from the Libyans led to barricades along Pennsylvania Avenue.) Anyway, the squirrels would eat straight out of my hand and I remained their staunch defenders. Until now.

Having ditched the vast responsibilities of First Street, I figured my narrow apartment balcony, anchored by four large pots of citrus; a smattering of herbs, violets, and succulents; and the prolific night-blooming cereus that's been with me since Bourbon Street, would be mostly maintenance free. And then the squirrels came. Leaping from electrical wires and the magnolia next door, they run brazenly along the wrought-iron railing, dive onto my satsuma and kumquat trees, and render them fruitless. Given my history with the peanuts, this is an almost literal case of biting the hand that feeds you. Though this is not the first time a fellow sentient being has betrayed my boundless love and trust, I'd rather come to expect such behavior from humans. From my furrier friends, it's somehow a whole lot more upsetting. Squirrel Nutkin, indeed.

Livestock of the Rich and Famous

WHEN I WAS GROWING UP, I SPENT A WHOLE LOT OF MY time down the street at the house of our neighbors, the Yarbroughs. Mrs. Yarbrough was an artist and an extraordinarily generous and funny woman who was also a psychic of sorts. She knew exactly when my grandmother (who had been in a coma for eleven years) was going to die, and everything she told me the first time she read my palm has happened pretty much the way she said it would. She and her husband had three girls whom I adored, and three boys who turned me on to the Allman Brothers and the Yardbirds and taught me such invaluable life skills as how to play poker and the best way to make a proper Yucca Flats (in a garbage can, with lots of gin and fresh citrus).

They also had a whole lot of animals. Inside, there was a box turtle who roamed around at his leisure, several boxes of guinea pigs (housed according to personality), and a parakeet who mostly flew free. Outside, there were cats too numerous to count and about a half dozen dogs, but what really set the Yarbroughs' place apart was their impressive collection of livestock. In those days on our road there were plenty of horses and cattle—our next-door neighbor owned hundreds of acres of pastureland behind our house, for example, but he was raising cattle to sell, not to keep as pets. The Yarbroughs, on the other hand, had no pasture or even any fences, just a regular yard of roughly three acres and a donkey tethered to the basketball hoop. I think the donkey might have been the first acquisition, but he was soon joined by a Brahman bull, a longhorn steer (when she bought it, Mrs. Y said simply that Dr. Yarbrough had always wanted one), a horse, and two Shetland ponies rescued from a rendering plant trailer.

None of them did much other than hang around near the driveway, but I think they gave Dr. and Mrs. Yarbrough a lot of pleasure, and after about three or four Yucca Flats, they became pretty entertaining to the rest of us as well. Mrs Y's motives were entirely altruistic and not just a little out there—and the animals certainly cost her a bit of money to maintain—but it turns out that if she had lived in Texas rather than Mississippi, her menagerie could have earned her money by giving her a break on her property taxes.

Now, on my frequent trips to Houston and Dallas, I have long noticed animals in unexpected places (the backyards of showy houses, in front of corporate offices), but I always thought that had more to do with Texas bravado or a special affection for longhorns, much like that of Dr. Yarbrough. But a few years ago, my friend the screenwriter Robert Harling was in Dallas filming a TV pilot based on the novel *Good Christian Bitches*, which is set in one of the city's more affluent neighborhoods, and he became extremely well versed in the ways of the Texas rich. It turns out that an "agricultural exemption" that dates back to 1966 enables home owners and corporations to save huge amounts in property taxes in exchange for activities as diverse as allowing a handful of pygmy goats to roam free or shooting a few deer so as to "prevent overuse of desirable plant species."

In the Fort Worth suburb of Westlake, for example, Boston-based Fidelity Investments has a 340-acre "corporate campus" that is home to its 401(k) customer service operations—as well as to twenty-four Texas longhorns. Four years ago, the *Wall Street Journal* uncovered the fact that the picturesque cattle earned an agricultural exemption for more than half of Fidelity's acreage, reducing the tax bill on that part of the property from $319,417 to a paltry $714.57. Likewise, Korean electronics maker Samsung cut taxes on 54 acres outside its Austin semiconductor plant from $21,080 to $135.68 by implementing a "wildlife plan" that included spraying for fire ants and installing ten birdhouses. Then there's John Benda, owner of Fuel City No. 2, a beloved truck stop in downtown Dallas where Interstate 30 and Interstate 35E meet. Benda's place sells tacos that have been named the best in the state by *Texas Monthly*, but now it's better known for the six longhorns and two donkeys out back. Not only does he get to dole out bumper stickers reading "Fuel City: The RANCH in Downtown Dallas," he reckons he saves about $30,000 a year.

As evidenced by Benda's eight animals, it doesn't take much to qualify for the tax break. All you have to do is prove that your property is being used "wholly or in part" for raising livestock, growing crops, or protecting wildlife—but the translations on all three items are pretty flexible. "Livestock" can include everything from the aforementioned pygmy goats to ostriches and emus; vegetation that allows indigenous birds to "cover from enemies" also qualifies. But a lot depends on the appraiser. One family in North Texas got turned down, not surprisingly, after trying to qualify with fireflies; another in Washington County applied for the exemption on the basis of some miniature donkeys, a species that gave the county's chief appraiser, Willy Dilworth, some qualms for not seeming farmlike enough. They "come up to you like a dog," he said, but he compromised by counting two or three of the little donkeys as a single horse.

For home buyers, the good news is that the exemptions are transferable. In a gated community in Flower Mound, a town just a few minutes from downtown Dallas, a 20,000-square-foot mansion is being offered for sale by the ex-wife of the oil tycoon who built it. It has six bedrooms and eight baths (including one with a musical flushing toilet), a "Moroccan" media room, two infinity pools, and a "secret" office behind a bookcase in the study. While I'm sure there must be some people to whom those lavish features are selling points, its biggest selling point may well be the fact that 9.4 of the property's 10.4 acres are covered under the agricultural exemption. Longhorns, horses, three mules, and a donkey roam around the place and are housed in a barn that includes a full bar.

Of course, no tax break is without risks—and I don't just mean in the form of trouble from the county appraiser or the state tax man. Our next-door neighbor who kept the cattle was notoriously lax about his fences, and his animals were forever getting loose. Once, a particularly ornery bull wandered into our backyard during the winter and fell right through our canvas pool cover. It took two days and all kinds of ropes and pulleys, not to mention a considerable amount of sweet-talking, to finally get him up the steps in the shallow end. And then our neighbor wanted us to pay him for the supposed trauma to the bull. If the Flower Mound manse is still on the market, prospective buyers should keep that in mind. Nothing spoils a lovely view of one of those infinity pools like an angry longhorn thrashing around.

Life Among
the Serpents

WHEN I GOT MARRIED IN MY MISSISSIPPI HOMETOWN, I wanted to ensure that the guests, many of whom were not from the South—or even America—understood where exactly it was that they were visiting. To that end, there was a dinner at Doe's Eat Place and another in an abandoned cotton gin. There were blues bands and soul bands and a festive pre-wedding lunch featuring pimento cheese sandwiches, ham biscuits, and fried chicken. Everybody went home with warm memories of my home state in particular and the South in general, and it wasn't until I got the pictures back that I realized I had given them even more local color than I'd thought.

It was a group shot from the lunch. People were gathered near the bar on the terrace, sipping Bloody Marys and laughing away, while beyond them a bank of French doors led inside to the feast. Maybe it was because the cypress doors were stained a dull brown; maybe it was the booze and the bonhomie. Either way, not a single guest noticed the six-foot-plus-long chicken snake coiled against one of the open doors.

I grew up in the middle of what is most often called simply "the Delta," the region in the northwest corner of the state which is in actuality the seven-thousand-square-mile diamond-shaped floodplain between the Mississippi and Yazoo rivers. Described by one early traveler as a "seething lush hell," it was, until well into the nineteenth century, the almost exclusive domain of panthers and bears, wild hogs and deer, alligators and, of course, snakes. Lured by the agricultural possibilities of some of the richest alluvial soil in the world, a handful of white settlers finally turned up in the 1820s and began hacking out fields and plantations from what Faulkner called "one jungle one brake one impassable density of brier and cane and vine interlocking the soar of gum and cypress and hickory and pinoak and ash."

Faulkner and his alter ego Ike McCaslin did not much approve of this process, but they may well get the last laugh. Like the bad child you can't turn your back on, "not even for *one* minute," all that vanquished wilderness keeps finding ways to fill up its old space, aided by a subtropical climate and an average of sixty inches of rainfall a year. The Delta's oak-hickory forest is, after all, at least sixteen thousand years old, and snakes are a whole lot older.

Depending on the source, Mississippi has up to fifty-five species of snakes, including nine venomous ones. (By comparison, Maine has one venomous snake, and it's found only in the southern part of the state.) I saw my first rattlesnake at four, when I almost stepped on it, running from our swimming pool to our house. At roughly the same age, my little brothers thought it adorable to bring home the baby water moccasins they found in the aptly named Rattlesnake Bayou, the nearby muddy stream that gave its name to the country road we lived on and that used to drain the whole town. Just last year, my best friend, Jessica Brent, was taking a bath when what she hopes was a harmless king snake (she never found it) took a peek at her from a stack of towels in the open linen closet.

Not that Louisiana, which I also call home, is much different. Roughly 450 venomous snakebites are reported annually, and after each one of the state's many floods, the Louisiana Department of Wildlife and Fisheries finds it necessary to remind residents to "seal gaps in windows and doors" and protect their "feet, ankles, and lower legs" against displaced snakes in general, and cottonmouths, copperheads, and canebrake rattlers in particular. Here too, there's a bayou named after a snake, the lordly Teche, derived from a Chitimacha word. According to Chitimacha legend, a giant snake attacked their villages, required a bunch of warriors to kill it, and left its carcass behind to decompose and fill with water. In commemoration, the city fathers of Breaux Bridge commissioned a twenty-foot granite snake sculpture that resides in its downtown park.

Morgan City, where the Teche empties into the Atchafalaya River, also pays tribute to the snake, but in the form of an unlikely event called the Snake Bite Triathlon, a swim, bike, and run through what the organizers refer to as the area's "beautiful swamp." Unbelievably, they also tout the "cypress trees, cool lake, and lots of snakes" that mark the location, but when I drove through Morgan City this past summer, none of that got my attention. An alligator had eased up onto Highway

90 and lost his head to the wheel of an oncoming car—a common sight down here in what we should only laughingly call civilization.

It has been more than a decade since my Mississippi wedding, but apparently the snakes continue to hang around the doorsteps. The last time I was home, my mother shrieked at me to "*shut the door!*" using additional language she reserves for dire occasions. For a refreshing change, the mosquitoes weren't swarming, so I was confused. "It's not the mosquitoes," she said. "It's the snakes." Snakes? Okay then, best to keep the door shut. There's a reason Mississippi State University's Extension Service has issued a downloadable pamphlet called "Reducing Snake Problems Around Homes."

The pamphlet makes the point that chemicals and fumigants have never effectively repelled snakes, and that home remedies concocted to keep rat snakes (the proper name of the chicken snake that attended my wedding lunch) at bay also have proved fruitless. These range from cayenne pepper spray to artificial skunk scent, but at our house we've always gone straight for the hoe. It is usually wielded by Frank Liger, the man in charge of my parents' house, garden, and pretty much every other aspect of their lives, but he is often forced to employ a helper to stay on top of the reptile situation. Frank reckons that hundreds of snakes reside in our six-acre yard and says that even when he is not actively looking for them, he runs into one or two a day.

The morning after my mother's meltdown, I found Frank and his helper with three black racers they'd cornered in a clump of bamboo. This is not easy to do. Described as curious (they will raise their heads out of the grass to check out what's

going on) and extremely quick (Frank calls them road run-
ners), they also eat stuff like rats and even other snakes. But
Frank was not interested in their more helpful qualities, he was
interested in keeping them out of the house. "When I see one,"
he said, "I try to do him as quick as I can." What about king
snakes? I asked. Their diet actually includes racers, and unlike
their prey, they don't often strike. "I don't trust them either,"
he said. "A snake is a snake. I'm not fooling with anything crawling on their stomachs. I know they are the devil."

Which brings us to another point: the resurgence in snake
handling in certain Pentecostal churches. In May 2012, a
preacher named Mark Wolford died of a bite inflicted by
a yellow timber rattlesnake during a service in West Virginia.
Though his father had died the same way twenty-nine years
earlier, and he himself had barely survived at least four bites
from copperheads, he remained undeterred, believing that if
you die, it simply means it's your time to go. It also means that
you provoked the hell out of a normally skittish snake—
copperheads in particular will try hard, according to my snake
book, to avoid confrontation. Prior to the fatal attack, Wolford
had passed the rattler around to members of his congregation;
when he sat down on the ground next to it, the snake put an
end to the proceedings by biting him on the thigh.

At this point, I have to say that I'm sort of with the snake.
According to my buddy Rob Ballinger, a biologist with the
Mississippi Fish and Wildlife Foundation, 75 percent of all
bites from venomous snakes occur when someone is trying to
kill or harass them. Being passed around to people shouting,
speaking in tongues, and jumping up and down in time to tam-
bourines must surely qualify as the latter. Still, the preachers

persist. Less than two months after attending Wolford's funeral, Andrew Hamblin, the twenty-one-year-old pastor at the Tabernacle Church of God in LaFollette, Tennessee, asked his county's commissioners to repeal a state law prohibiting the ownership of venomous snakes. The commissioners quashed the resolution, and the law, enacted in 1947 after snakebites killed five people in churches during a two-year period, still stands.

Hamblin, who has been bitten four times, ignored the vote, posted news of an upcoming service on Facebook, and allowed a news crew to film it. Before the service began, a church member pulled three copperheads out of a wooden box, swung them over his head, and handed them to Hamblin, who raised his free hand in prayer. "My main thing is to see lost people saved," he said, "but I would love to do it under the anointment of God with two rattlers in my hand."

All this stuff goes back to a little-known passage in the Gospel of Mark, which reads in part, "They shall take up serpents; and if they drink any deadly thing, it shall not hurt them." I'm no theologian, but I'm not sure that's the first passage referring to snakes I'd zero in on. For one thing, most biblical historians say the passage wasn't even in the first Greek versions of Mark. More important, the serpent was identified as the guy you want to seriously avoid pretty much from the get-go. In case anyone needs reminding, my aforementioned friend Jessica and her two sisters, Eden and Bronwynne (aka the Brent Sisters), recently released an excellent CD of their mother Carole's songs, one of which contains the following instructive lyrics: "Adam and Eve had a real nice pad in a kingdom by the sea./Along came a snake, a rake on the take, and the landlord demanded the key."

Temptation, as we know, strikes everyone, even in this seemingly off-putting area. A roundup of recent deadly snakebites in our region includes one in Chattanooga that occurred when the victim was trying to determine a copperhead's sex and another in Putnam County, Florida, when a fire marshal reached for a rattler who sought refuge under a shed after his neighbor shot at it. I am fairly sure I don't know anybody that crazy, which is why we didn't incur the wrath of the chicken snake that day at the party. My snake book says that rat snakes are "ill-tempered" and "will readily defend themselves" when provoked. In our case, no defense was necessary, since we were all too busy eating and drinking to notice the thing, much less provoke it. Also, I think the snake was just biding his time. The species has been known to climb trees as high as forty feet in search of birds and the contents of their nests. As it happened, the lunch tables' very chic centerpieces were abandoned nests collected from the wilds of a typical Delta backyard. The nests were empty, of course, but the snake didn't know that. What he knows is that he and the birds (and the bears and the deer and the gators and on and on) still own the place. The rest of us are very recent visitors.

Mastering the Hunt

I COME FROM A STATE, MISSISSIPPI (AND AN AREA WITHIN it, the Delta), that is widely known for its passion for outdoor pursuits, chief among them hunting. According to a recent survey, Mississippi boasts more than ten hunters per square mile, and I swear I think I know at least half of them. I have feasted on countless carcasses of their venison and duck, I've been presented with such unlikely (but much loved) tokens of affection as turkey feet and feathers, I've been a guest at many a festive field breakfast to mark the opening day of dove season. Arguably the most famous hunt on American soil occurred just down the road from where I grew up—the 1902 bear hunt at which President Theodore Roosevelt refused to shoot his cornered quarry, an act that gave birth to the now classic teddy bear.

It's embarrassing, then, that hunting to me has been all about breakfast casseroles and Bloody Marys. While I'm happy to avail myself of the spoils of other people's wars, the only thing

I have successfully aimed at and hit was a rusted beer can atop a fence post.

There was one misguided duck-hunting foray during my college years with my lifelong running buddies Anne and Elizabeth McGee and my Georgetown roommate, Anne Flaherty. The latter, who hailed from Boston, was then a Delta novice, and it was decided by the McGee sisters' maternal uncle Jody Gee (yes, Anne Ross Gee married Burrell McGee and good things happened all around) that she should be schooled in our native pursuits. Since he had never thought to school the rest of us, we were singularly ill prepared when we piled into Elizabeth's Ford Granada to make the trek to Carroll County for the afternoon hunt. In order to look good for the ducks (or, more to the point, our fellow hunters), Anne McGee plugged a set of electric rollers into the car lighter and began to roll her hair. I am pretty sure some beers were consumed. When we got there, Jody had us practice on some Schlitz cans, and we were feeling pretty competent until we got into the boats. That's when we realized that the ducks were far, far away, plus they moved. Not that there were very many of them. Jody had made the grave error of splitting us between two vessels, which meant that we had to yell to make conversation and/or ask for the flask to be passed. In the end, everyone gave up. When we gratefully disembarked, Jody's friend Herman thought it would be hilarious to impersonate the game warden and demand to see our hunting licenses, which of course we didn't have. Given that the rest of Jody's companions were named Perchmouth, Rubber Lips, and Fat Cat, we had to wonder if Anne's grooming efforts had been worth the trouble. Either way, I can safely say that none of us has endeavored to repeat the experience.

Not until almost forty years later, that is, when I participated in two life-changing hunts. The first was in February, a re-creation of the momentous bear hunt, organized by Hank Burdine, master of the hunt—and pretty much everything else to do with grand times and big fun—at our friend Howard Brent's Panther Tract, a 4,400-acre wilderness paradise near the Yazoo River. In Roosevelt's day, thousands of black bears roamed the Mississippi Delta, which was then also home to enormous swaths of bottomland forests. But by the 1930s, the desire to get at the Delta's fertile soil meant that most of the forests had been cleared and the swamps drained, and the bear population had dwindled to a tragic dozen. Now protected, with its habitat on the mend, the black bear currently numbers more than 150 and is happily on the rise.

Needless to say, we would not be going after the fragile bear, but wild hogs, which have all but taken over the state. For historical purposes the hunt would be much like the bear hunts of old, in which hunters on horseback chased hounds on the scent and often literally jumped into the fray, killing the bear with a knife or a pistol rather than a rifle (better to protect the prized dogs). I get that the visceral nature of things may well gross some people out, but it keeps things authentic and highly sporting, and we'd also be performing a service of sorts. The hogs are an extraordinarily expensive nuisance, eating up pretty much everything in their paths, including the levees, the crops, and the Natchez Trace Parkway. A single hog consumes an astonishing ton of food per year, and they are also super busy. They give birth as early as six months of age, and they're seriously good at outsmarting people.

All this is to say there's no season for wild hogs—I know

farmers who hire helicopters from which to shoot them from the sky at night. While folks insist that their meat makes excellent eating, there aren't enough diners in the world to reduce the population by 70 percent a year, which is what it would take just to keep them stable. But these pesky problems were far beyond our purview on the glorious, crisp morning of the hunt. For the occasion, Hank had managed to assemble most of the descendants of the participants in the original hunt, including: Roosevelt's great-great-grandson Simon Roosevelt, a devoted conservationist and avid hunter; Billy Percy, great-grandson of Roosevelt's friend Senator LeRoy Percy; Harley Metcalfe III, who brought the knife his grandfather Clive Metcalfe used during a second (more successful) hunt with Roosevelt; and Huger Foote, the photographer son of Civil War historian Shelby Foote and great-grandson of Roosevelt's hunting partner, also named Huger. (The decision by Foote and the president to leave the blind for refreshment was what led to the tethered bear—when the beast was chased through, there was no one on hand to take a shot. The fearless guide, Holt Collier, wrestled the bear to save his dogs before tying him to a tree.)

The event began the night before with a huge bonfire, lots of guitar playing, and a feast that included a (domestic) pork roast. At daybreak, dozens of hunters on horseback arrived, the dogs were let out of their pens, and the chase was on. True to form, the hogs proved elusive, though at least a half dozen were dispatched. I was proud to note that there were as many female hunters as male, though I was not among them, content to view the proceedings from the back of a four wheeler. Still, it must be said that I was not just a little jealous of my pal Melody Golding, the good-looking and gifted horsewoman who's written a book about hog hunting and who sported a formidable handmade knife on her hip. I also learned that more than freezer fodder can come from having a hunting-obsessed loved one. Harley Metcalfe's ever-stylish wife, Gayden, wore not a knife but a beautiful pair of gold-capped boar's teeth on a chain around her neck. Mostly, though, I was just happy to be there. The setting was stunning, the company good, and the opportunity to mark the hunt held 115 years prior in such a respectful and celebratory manner was not lost on any of us. Thus it was that the aforementioned Mr. Metcalfe persuaded me to go deeper into my exploration of hunting's pleasures. For years I'd ribbed Harley and his fellow turkey hunters about engaging in a practice I'd always perceived as the worst kind of torture. As anyone who has ever met me will attest, I'm the most impatient person in the world, and for the life of me I could not fathom the allure of sitting stock-still, forbidden to make a sound except with a turkey call, waiting—and waiting—for hours on end for a turkey to pass by. But I've known Harley all my life, and he's an intuitive fellow, so I figured he might be onto something.

As it turned out, our timing might have been better. The night before our 3:30 A.M. wake-up call, Hank's beautiful daughter Alden got married on the banks of Lake Washington. By the time we reluctantly tore ourselves from the festivities, we had an hour-long trek before us to Catfish Point, the hunting club where Harley keeps a very chic "cabin" on stilts and another of God's wonders: twelve thousand acres on one of the Mississippi River's most stunning bends. After a quick biscuit breakfast, we repaired to the clubhouse, where a dozen additional members had gathered to draw for their spots. Despite the abominable (to me) hour, it was a jolly group, with muddy Labradors running all about and bits of gossip (there had been two more weddings in town) exchanged, and I remembered how much the familiar bullshit patter of Delta men and dogs thoroughly restores my soul.

As we walked out, the only sounds were those of our feet making their way through the brush and the earliest of the birds. After we situated ourselves against the trunk of an exceedingly wide tree, my first test arrived in the form of a mosquito buzzing away between my right eye and my mesh camo mask. When I moved to brush it away, Harley made his own almost imperceptible move to stop me and, miraculously, I did. We made occasional hushed conversation, watched the light come up and change, listened to the next round of birds. Every now and then Harley demonstrated his prowess with the turkey call, and when seven turkeys paraded right in front of us, I could hardly contain my excitement. A disgusted Harley explained that they were jakes, too young to shoot and too occupied by a nearby female to get out of the way.

Before I knew it, hours had passed. We moved to a blind where we heard a gobbler respond to Harley's imitation of a love-starved hen. We waited, feeling him behind us, but we were facing the wrong way and dared not move. Finally, something spooked him and we called it a day. Now, Harley is an excellent hunter who every year bags the club limit before heading off to Texas, where he shoots the limit there. I knew he was not happy about being bested by the bearded bird (which he got the next day), and on the way back into town he apologized for the lack of action. What he didn't realize was that I'd seen plenty. In a matter of hours, he'd turned me on to an experience that had taught me the art of Zen and made me profoundly grateful to be part of the very earth we'd been sitting on. Next year he's vowed to teach me to shoot, and it's a skill set I'd at long last be proud to have. Still, I doubt the next time I'm against that tree, I'll bother to raise a weapon. There are far too many other things to do.

Part Three

Southern
Sustenance

A Delta Original

ONE OF THE THINGS I'VE ALWAYS LIKED ABOUT THE MIS-
sissippi Delta in general, and my hometown, Greenville, specifically, is that there's always been a surprisingly cosmopolitan
mix of cultures and nationalities. When Greenville was incorporated (again) just after the Civil War (during which it was
destroyed by Sherman's troops after the Siege of Vicksburg), the
first elected mayor was Jewish, as were the owners of the first
businesses to open and the founder of the first school. Since
1900, the majority of the citizenry have been African American, but there is also a sizable Syrian population, as well as large
numbers of Chinese and Southern Italians. What we have never
had in any significant amount are Mexican Americans.

Thus it likely came as no small surprise to the world at
large a few years ago when our much-loved former mayor, the
late Chuck Jordan, issued a proclamation declaring Greenville the Hot Tamale Capital of the World. The ceremony on the

steps of city hall was followed a few months later by the first annual Delta Hot Tamale Festival, which featured twenty-odd vendors whose wares I was lucky enough to sample in my official capacity as a judge. Most of the five thousand folks who turned up appeared to be fairly local, so they knew better than to expect a mariachi band or the comparatively bland and crumbly Mexican tamales that bear little resemblance to the moist, delicious, and highly seasoned Delta versions.

The latter are a predominantly African-American delicacy, but the ones I've been eating all my life, from Doe's Eat Place, get even more complicated. Doe Signa Sr. was a first-generation Sicilian immigrant whose now landmark restaurant began life as a juke that also sold take-out spaghetti and tamales to his mostly African-American neighbors. When his son, Doe Jr., married his wife, "Sug" (short for "Sugar"), he warned him never to reveal the tamale recipe to her lest she leave him for someone else with whom she might share the formula. More than thirty years later, in 2007, the couple took the stage at Lincoln Center with the rest of the family after Doe's was named an "American Classic" by the James Beard Foundation, and Sug described the atmosphere of the restaurant, which remains refreshingly unchanged: "People come together, never meet a stranger, it's the American way."

Much the same could be said of the creation of the Delta tamale itself, about which there is much speculation but little hard info, though the good folks at the Southern Foodways Alliance have made a valiant effort. The shortest and most likely version is that it dates back to the early twentieth century, when migrant workers were occasionally brought in from Mexico to pick cotton alongside the local African Americans, who would certainly have been familiar with the two main ingredients, cornmeal and pork. Another theory has the Italian population traveling down the river and doing their own recipe trading with migrant workers.

Versions of both could well be the case, a point articulated in one of the oral histories conducted by the SFA's Amy Evans Streeter as part of the organization's Hot Tamale Trail project. "Basically, the Delta was built up on a lot of people who were just travelers going from one destination to another," Larry Lee, a former salesman at Greenville's Hot Tamale Heaven, told Streeter. "That's how the people melted here. . . . And from that, you get all kinds of cultures and ideas—you know, you share with me, I share with you. And before long, what can I tell you? Something came out of it and the tamale was one of those things."

Whatever its origin, a Delta tamale is smaller than its Mexican counterpart and is usually made with plain white cornmeal as opposed to the finer masa. The filling is almost always well-spiced pork or beef, and the tamales themselves are simmered in liquid rather than steamed, a process that creates a tasty "juice" that bathes them in their shucks and keeps them moist. By 1928, their popularity among both blacks and whites was such that the Reverend Moses Mason recorded a song called "Molly Man" that included the lyrics "Good times is comin'/Don't you see the sign?/White folks standin' round here, spending many dimes" (on the tamales that were then thirty cents a dozen). Eight years later Robert Johnson's slightly more suggestive "They're Red Hot" quotes the same price, which is a little less than what my father says he paid during his childhood in Caruthersville, Missouri, not far north of the Delta on the Mississippi: "You could buy them on the street, three for a dime, or you could roll the dice with the man, who always won. I grew up thinking they were a product of the Mississippi River rather than Mexico."

My own relationship with tamales began at an even younger age—there's a photo of my mother, eight and a half months pregnant with me, sitting on the wooden front steps of Doe's. Since then I've eaten enough of them to make me fairly confident as a judge, but still, it's a complicated business. My fellow judges (including my dear friend and *Garden & Gun* colleague Roy Blount, Jr., who was kind enough to make the trip) were given badges featuring dancing tamales and a lengthy orientation session during which we received guidance on how to score categories ranging from presentation to tenderness—a quality we were told "speaks for itself."

There was an artisanal division and a commercial division, dessert tamales (including a weirdly delicious strawberry version made by the talented Antoinette Turner, of Drew, to whom I gave high marks), and a decidedly un-Delta tamale filled with butter beans and chicken from a bird its maker, "Papa Doc," claimed to have recently killed himself. The top three winners in the artisanal category were makers of classic versions from Greenville, as was the Grand Champion, Mr. Gerald Jefferson, who was so overwhelmed by the crowds trying to buy his tamales that I never got to interview him about his technique.

There was plenty of other stuff to do, though. As at all good festivals, there was a parade and music (including performances by Greenville's own Steve Azar and my pal Raymond Longoria, whose family once owned a tamale stand), a hot tamale tale-telling "front porch" anchored by my buddy the inimitable Hank Burdine, and, of course, a Miss Hot Tamale, a stunning St. Joseph High School sophomore named Jade Mixon, whose ingenious (and startlingly attractive) dress was made entirely of corn shucks dusted with a hint of gold glitter. Naming the first queen was a no-brainer—she was Florence Signa, the late Doe Sr.'s beloved sister-in-law, who still works at the restaurant three or four nights a week and who greeted her subjects in a corn-shuck crown.

There was also a tamale-eating contest, won by a brave soul named Detric Boldien, who consumed twenty-five in five minutes. I was impressed with his achievement—he had to unwrap them, after all—but when I relayed his score to my friend W. Hodding Carter, whom I've convinced to accompany me to next year's fest, he scoffed. Like me, Hodding grew up in Greenville, where he consumed a whole lot of hots. He's also an intrepid sort who wrote one book about replicating the Lewis and Clark expedition and another about training to qualify for the Olympics in swimming at forty-two. More than twenty years ago, he wrote a piece for *Outside* magazine about coming in second at an oyster-eating contest at a seafood festival in Louisiana's Lafourche Parish. That particular festival no longer exists, but I went to it once, the year after Hodding competed. It was held, for reasons I'll never understand, in July. The heat—and the stench—was brutal. Hodding, who was then living in New York, had trained mostly in the air-conditioned oyster bars at Grand Central Station and the Plaza Hotel and was no match for an oil-field worker named Danny Vining, who ate 151 oysters in fifteen minutes. Still, Hodding came close—his score of 136 would have been higher but for the fact that the 136th oyster stayed on his fork for a full two minutes before he could force himself to swallow it. Plus, when time was called, Danny still had his last sixteen oysters in his mouth.

Hodding is already pumped up for next year's contest and has asked me to warn Mr. Boldien that he's not holding onto his title. A little competition will be exciting, and there'll be more stuff too, including a food writers' symposium. We'll have to come up with something to talk about other than how the tamale made its way to the Delta, because I'm pretty sure we'll never know. I'm sticking with what Mr. Lee told Amy Streeter: "The best way I can sum it up is that you're not from the Delta if you know nothing of tamales. It's that simple. It's the levee, it's the blues, it's the tamale."

Good to the Bone

A FEW YEARS AGO I WENT OUT TO DINNER IN NEW Orleans with some friends, and the talk turned, as it so often does, to food. Specifically to the singular glories of fried chicken, which we all apparently wished we were eating instead of the grilled salmon that sat, rather reproachfully, on our plates. I can talk all day about chicken and was gearing up to debate the finer points of, say, lard vs. Crisco (lard), garlic powder or not (yes), when one of the women at the table piped up that her favorite part of the chicken happened to be the bones.

Now, I know we Southerners are famous for eating a lot of stuff most people don't. Dirt, poke sallet, and Goo Goo Clusters are just a few things that come immediately to mind. But I had never heard of anyone not only eating but favoring the bones of a fried chicken.

"Bones?" I asked brightly, even though what I was thinking was "Are you out of your mind? The last time my dog ate chicken bones I had to take him to the vet." But she looked at me as if I were the one who was crazy, as if I might be the only person in the world who didn't know the secret of their goodness. "Yes," she said, "the bones," adding that she sucked the marrow out of them first. For the second time in less than a minute, I was floored. I am all about beef and veal marrow—in stews, spread on toast with a little sea salt, scooped out of a hunk of osso buco with a proper silver marrow spoon. But I feel sure that if I had ever bothered to think about it, I would have assumed that the amount of marrow in a chicken's skinny bones would be negligible. This is where I would be wrong. "You haven't lived until you've sucked out the marrow," she told me with, I swear, a faintly glazed look in her eyes. And then she added the kicker: "And then of course there is the gristle, et cetera."

I should point out here that this woman is not a figure out of a Walker Evans photograph. She is smart and attractive and funny and well off enough not to have to resort to bones and gristle to keep from going hungry. So when she uttered the words "gristle, et cetera," my mouth must have dropped open, because she felt the need to reassure me that eating a chicken in its entirety, especially the "crispy wings," is not a big deal. "It's just like eating shrimp shells," she said. I don't eat those either, but in the end I had to admire the thoroughness and gusto with which this woman dispatched her bird. Plus, I came across a song lyric by an Austin-based singer/songwriter I like a lot named Bob Schneider that attests to the fact that the bones are fairly easy to eat. In "Come with Me Tonight," there's a line about "Larry," who "Always gets it wrong/His heart's as soft as chicken bone."

Schneider's is not the only song that mentions chicken—or bones, either, for that matter. There's a great Danny Barker song, popularized by Johnny Mercer, called "Save the Bones for Henry Jones," in which "Henry don't eat no meat." My friend Jimmy Phillips has a song called "Gnawing Bone," in which a guy gets a clue that his woman has left him when he comes home to an open door and an empty house: "The whole place smells like pork chops/But ain't no pig meat on the stove/Just some cold grease in the skillet/And one low-down gnawing bone." Jimmy also wrote "Fried Chicken," which has to be the best song ever written on the subject. It mentions neither marrow nor gristle, but it comes close with a line about "All that knuckle-sucking goodness just looking back at me" and goes on to explain that "Full awareness is heightened/When the grease goes to your brain." Eden Brent covers "Fried Chicken" on her *Mississippi Number One* CD, and whenever she plays it live, people go just as crazy for it as they do for the real thing.

There are very few people who don't go crazy over fried chicken, a point not lost on the editors of *Bon Appétit*, who surely boosted the magazine's February 2012 newsstand sales by putting a gorgeous golden drumstick on the cover, along with a line touting the "41 Soulful Recipes from America's New Food Capital" inside. While I'm all for promoting chicken and Southern food in general, and I subscribe to *Bon Appétit*, I do have a couple of tiny quibbles. One, in its recipe, the chicken is batter fried, which is okay—maybe—if you want to eat it cold the next day for a picnic. Otherwise it should be tossed in a paper bag with flour and seasonings, period. No egg ever need enter the process.

Two, I sort of disagree with that word *new*. When were we

not the nation's food capital, really? Let us all remember that while the Puritans were munching on what the historian David Hackett Fischer calls their "canonical dish" of cold baked beans, we were down here supping on chicken fricassee made with "a pint of red claret, a pint of oysters and a dozen egg yolks." At no point in history would I rather have eaten anywhere else, but to be fair, *Bon Appétit* is referring to our current crop of hot chefs and the fact that the rest of the country has finally caught up to our obsessions with ham and pimento cheese and small-batch bourbons and things like "house-made" pickles, which is pretty much what we've been eating all along.

With the exception of the fried chicken, there are some excellent recipes in the issue, including the brilliant Charleston chef Mike Lata's swanky chicken and dumplings and my friend Martha Foose's luscious-looking coconut cake, which is enlivened by a healthy dose of Southern Comfort. (The editors of the magazine clearly understood the importance of whiskey to our cuisine—there is also a braised brisket with a bourbon peach glaze and a banana cream pie with salty bourbon caramel.) Martha's cake is one that I would actually make. A cake I would not make is the coconut cake with saffron cream garnish from *Food & Wine*'s Southern food issue a couple of years earlier.

In that issue, "50 Best Recipes from the New South," the editors decided to "update" some "classics" by attempting to make them healthy, a sobering exercise that resulted in a recipe for "smoky shrimp and grits" that substituted canola oil for butter, as well as a pairing of sausage gravy with whole-wheat biscuits, which is just weird. Some classics are better left unupdated, so I have been reaching way back instead. The recent

Dining with the Washingtons: Historic Recipes, Entertaining, and Hospitality from Mount Vernon includes a fine chicken fricassee recipe, and at Charleston's now sadly shuttered Heirloom Books, which was my favorite culinary bookstore, I found another treasure, *Pearl's Kitchen: An Extraordinary Cookbook*, by Pearl Bailey. Bailey was one of my childhood idols—I loved to hear her sing and talk about her husband, the Italian-American jazz drummer Louis Bellson, on *The Tonight Show*. She had a ton of soul, and I should have known she'd be an excellent cook and storyteller.

A recipe for pork chops and green apples, for example, starts off with the line: "I had a dinner a few nights ago that was more exciting, actually sexier, than a best-selling novel. What, you may ask, does sex have to do with food? Darlin', I am not going into that right now. Just let me tell you that what got me so excited was pork chops, buttered rice, and Mama's cabbage." She reports that she served more cabbage and rice with Baked Sole Spontaneous "and the whole family had a real ball." She rails against too-thin aluminum nonstick pans and prefers butter or lard to margarine, which she loathes.

Pearl grew up in Philadelphia, but she was born in Newport News, Virginia, and her mother, a constant figure in the book, clearly knew her way around a kitchen. Not only did Ella Mae Bailey cook "the best fried chicken in the world" every Sunday morning, she also went to the chicken man to "blow the feathers back" and choose her own live bird. Like my friend, Pearl was most fond of the wings, but she "liked the necks too and sometimes the gizzard" because "there was an old wives' tale that said if you ate the chicken gizzard you would become pretty."

Pearl was as passionate about chicken as my gristle-loving, marrow-sucking friend, but then Pearl was passionate about everything. At one point she wrote, "I don't like to say that my kitchen is actually a religious place, but I would say that if I were a voodoo priestess, I would conduct my rituals there." Let's not forget that a lot of them involve the bones of a chicken.

Bizarre Foods

In 2014, THE INTREPID FOOD WRITER, JOURNALIST, novelist, poet, memoirist, and (whew) much-lauded humorist Calvin Trillin journeyed to my hometown of Greenville, Mississippi, to do a piece for the *New Yorker* on the second annual Delta Hot Tamale Festival. I'd implored him and he'd relented, but before he left town, he tapped his notebook and said that if he managed to get a story out of what was inside, he'd nominate his own self for a MacArthur genius grant. He got one, of course (a piece, not the award, but he's already won the Thurber Prize for American Humor), and it was terrific and funny and full of good stuff on tamales and Delta culture, both of which he'd long known a little bit about. During his five-day stay, he'd gamely sampled fried tamales, vegetarian tamales, a tamale pie, and the rather more highbrow offerings of the competing celebrity chefs, including New Orleans's Donald Link and Stephen Stryjewski, and Michael Hudman and Andy Ticer, who own five restaurants in Memphis. Then, on the day of the fest itself, a vendor offered him a more recent example of Delta food culture: a Kool-Aid pickle, also known as a Koolickle, a Day-Glo-colored delicacy made by draining the brine from a gallon jar of dill pickles and replacing it with double-strength Kool-Aid and a whole lot of sugar.

Trillin may well be the funniest human being I've ever met; he is also an exceptionally polite man. So after a couple of bites, when pressed for an opinion of the rather alarming cherry-red item in his hand, he "took refuge," he wrote, "in the initialism I.C.P., Interesting Culinary Phenomenon."

Clearly, Trillin was not mad for the Koolickle. And while I'm famously big on promoting Delta culture in all its glorious forms, I'm not entirely sold on it myself. But we are in the minority. As early as 2007, John T. Edge, the director of the Southern Foodways Alliance, wrote in the *New York Times* that the popularity of the Koolickle had spread beyond the Delta— where it was mostly sold out of people's kitchens (much like hot tamales), at neighborhood stores, and at blues-festival food stands—to cities as far away as Dallas and St. Louis. He also reported that the Indianola, Mississippi–based convenience-store chain DoubleQuick had applied for a trademark on the term *Koolickle*, coined by the stores' director of food service. Since then, the application seems to have lapsed, and some DoubleQuicks now tout the same product under the name Pickoolas. Either way, to quote Edge, "Depending on your palate and perspective, they are either the worst thing to happen to pickles since plastic brining barrels or a brave new taste sensation to be celebrated."

The latter is a happy fate that has greeted more than one I.C.P. I'll have to ask Trillin, but I feel like when an I.C.P. becomes so entrenched that chefs start riffing on it with "gourmet" versions, it no longer qualifies for the initials. At any rate, it was bound to happen. Hayden Hall, an artist and chef in Clarksdale, Mississippi, made an upscale version of the Koolickle for some members of the Association of Food Journalists a couple of years ago that by all reports was a big hit. Hall has chops—he worked at Wolfgang Puck's the Source in Washington, D.C., and Susan Spicer's Bayona in New Orleans before returning home to the Delta—and he emphasizes the Koolickle's sweet-and-sour flavor combo rather than its scary color, which he avoids by not actually using Kool-Aid. Instead, he heats up homemade lemonade and adds his own homemade dills along with a handful of rosemary or mint or basil from his garden, and lets everything steep before chilling. The formula, he says, keeps the pickle "in the 'ade' world" without being too outré. Next he's thinking of adding vodka to the mix, an excellent idea that will take the pickles firmly out of the I.C.P. camp and turn them into convenient alcohol delivery systems along the lines of the now classic vodka-spiked watermelon.

When I was a kid, dill pickles were just dill pickles and sat among the more bizarre or just plain gross items lined up in gallon jars on the wooden counters of gas stations and grocery stores—things like pickled eggs and pickled pigs' feet and lips and hocks, as well as the occasional pickled sausages called Red Hots that are dyed the same scary red shade as the Koolickles of today. But just as Hall has fancified the Kool-Aid pickle, the whole nose-to-tail movement—the wildly popular trend in which chefs allow no part of an animal to go to waste—has moved the pig parts out of the gas-station jar and onto the up-scale plate.

In 2006, Hudman and Ticer got turned on to nose-to-tail cooking when they spent a year in Italy prior to opening the first of their five restaurants, Andrew Michael, and attended a family pig killing. They remember the uncle procuring the brains to scramble up with some eggs while the grandmother, in her bedroom slippers, stirred the blood to keep it from coagulating. "We figured we could do the same in our kitchen," Ticer says, and they did. The menu at Andrew Michael has featured cakes made of the meat of braised trotters (otherwise known as feet) as well as a localized homage to Raymond Blanc's trotter stuffed with morels and sweetbreads (but because they're Memphis boys and not a French chef camped out in England, the sweetbreads were barbecued first). Across the street at Hog & Hominy, they serve a pig's tail that's braised, fried, and sauced in the manner of buffalo chicken wings.

Porcellino's, another of the duo's establishments, boasts a full-time butcher and meat curer as well as a nine-hundred-square-foot-plus walk-in refrigerator containing whole carcasses of cows, lambs, and pigs, very little of which goes unused. Fried bits of pig ear lend some tasty crunch to the popular brussels sprouts salad, and smoked ears are turned into the occasional terrine. Now that they are finally happy with the texture of the pickled ears, they plan on frying them in strips and serving them in a mason jar along with some ranch dressing enlivened by Calabrian chiles, tarragon, and basil. "It'll be sort of like a serving of fries with ketchup," Hudman says, adding that if you cut the ears into long enough strips, "they'll curl up a bit—they're really pretty."

Though the beauty of the slightly curled length of pig ear might elude a lot of people, those same folks will most likely be tempted by the ranch dressing, the sauce of choice for all manner of fried stuff, including the tamale. Likewise, the ears, says Hudman, will serve as "a vehicle to get ranch to your face." Porcellino's already has a similar vehicle on the menu, sliced pickled tomatillos, fried and served with an especially addictive ranch made with mascarpone cheese. That dish is an inspired tribute to a former I.C.P., the fried dill pickle chip, an item that long ago made the transition to I.D.P., or Insanely Delicious Phenomenon. (Hudman, who says he'll "mow down a basket of fried pickle chips in a second," agrees with my initialism.)

The fried dill chip is said to have been invented sometime in the early 1970s in—where else?—the Delta, near Tunica, Mississippi, at the Hollywood Café. Opened in 1969 and immortalized in the Marc Cohn hit "Walking in Memphis," the Hollywood fries its much-copied pickles in beer batter seasoned with cayenne pepper and chile powder, and I can attest that they're worth traveling many miles to enjoy. The thinness of the chip is key, as is the chip itself—at Pickle's restaurant in Seaside, Florida, they serve batter-fried dill spears, a grave error (though I do recommend the frozen margaritas).

Ticer and Hudman say they have no interest in doing a take on a pickled egg, especially not the red-dyed version, another countertop I.C.P. of old, but Emeril Lagasse has a recipe for pickled eggs and beets that no less an arbiter than Martha Stewart posted on her website. The adventurous Hall has boiled and steeped eggs in red wine for color, but no chef I talked to had any interest in spiffing up pickled pork lips or hocks, the fatty knuckles of the animal. For the real, unadulterated versions, you can head online to the Pickled Store if your neighborhood market or childhood gas station has, perhaps understandably, given up on them. The site offers up no fewer than eight varieties of pickled eggs and five of pigs' feet, but also lips and hocks, put up for three generations by a company called Matt & Dana in Amite, Louisiana.

The Pickled Store bills pig lips as "one of the cornerstones of pickled pork products" and laments, with a seemingly straight face, that they're "getting harder and harder to find." Despite a marketing pitch that claims "the best thing about pig lips is that you can kiss 'em before you eat 'em," neither Hudman nor Ticer nor Stryjewski, chef/owner at Cochon and Cochon Butcher, has any intention of going near them. Stryjewski says the lips, disconnected from the hog, colored a deep red or pink, and grinning out from the sides of the jar, are the one pork piece he wants nothing to do with. "They scare me." But the thing about the varied taste buds of our ever-surprising fellow country-men is that one man's unnerving I.C.P. is another man's beloved snack. Judging by the testimonials on Matt & Dana's pickled lips page, the company might live to see another generation. "A sleeper," Skip writes. "Really good, unexpected, and now a staple." Mindy agrees, calling the lips "a very nice experience! Strong porky flavor and wonderful texture." Susie from Ar-kansas is even more effusive: "I'd have to give these pig lips the loudest Woooooo, Pig! Sooie! call ever." Still, to play it safe, the company might want to consider branching out into the brave new world of Kool-Aid pickles.

A Tasteful
Send-off

IN APRIL 2014 IN NEW ORLEANS, MICKEY EASTERLING,
a woman described in various obituaries as a "philanthropist and
party giver," attended her own funeral. I realize it's true that we
all, in one form or another, attend our own funerals, but Easterling was not lying quietly in a coffin or residing in a tasteful
urn. She was sitting upright, on a platform erected for the occasion, decked to the nines in a big black hat and a hot-pink
feather boa, a cigarette holder in one manicured hand and a
Waterford crystal flute of champagne in the other.

The event, held in the grand Italianate lobby of the newly
restored Saenger Theatre on Canal Street, was attended by more
than a thousand people and made the news as far away as Ottawa
and London, where people were riveted by the details, most of
which had been carefully planned by the, um, hostess. Among
the tidbits reported: the items atop the wrought-iron table next to
the garden seat in which she sat (champagne bucket containing

an open bottle of Veuve Clicquot, coffee-table book on hats, pack of American Spirit cigarettes); the ferns and pots of white phalaenopsis orchids flanking the "stage" to approximate her own backyard pool patio; the fact that she wore her favorite jeweled brooch (spelling out the word *bitch*); and her age, eighty-three, which seemed a tad unfair since most of the articles also quoted one of her trademark lines ("Age is a number, and mine's unlisted").

There was no program, just a jazz combo on a balcony above and a whole lot of people approaching the "garden area" and raising their glasses (and their camera phones) to the figure before them. "It was a very pleasant effect," her friend, the Tennessee Williams scholar Kenneth Holditch, told a reporter with the Canadian Broadcasting Corporation. "At first I hesitated to even go look, but when I did . . . it was not unseemly." Sammy Steele, who did her makeup, went further: "She looks wonderful. She is a living legend, even in death."

I will have to take their word for it, though the large color photo on the front page of the *New Orleans Advocate*, the city's new daily, was perhaps a tiny bit jarring, if not flat-out grotesque. Still, Easterling was not the first New Orleans "legend" to make a splashy exit. When Ernie K-Doe (the rhythm and blues singer most famous for the 1961 hit "Mother-in-Law") died in 2001, his widow, Antoinette, commissioned an effigy, made from a department store mannequin, so that he could remain a presence, seated on a throne in their nightclub, the Mother-in-Law Lounge. Dressed in an ever-changing selection of his former performing outfits, the look-alike K-Doe—in real life he had often referred to himself as the Emperor of the Universe—was also occasionally taken out for public appearances by his wife before she died, in 2009. Then, two years ago, there was Lionel Batiste, the bass drummer of the Treme Brass Band, who attended his wake leaning against a street lamp, wearing a hat and suit and his familiar watch, whistle, and rings. That had been the doing of his son, who had promised his father that he would "send [him] off good" and enlisted the help of the funeral director Louis Charbonnet. "You have to think outside the box," Charbonnet told the *Times-Picayune*. "And so he's outside the box. We didn't want him to be confined to his casket."

Putting aside the fact that this seemingly growing trend of dead people sitting and standing around all over town is getting to be unsettling, I was interested in Easterling's painstaking orchestration of her own departure. There was, for example, the dress she wore by Leonard, a French fashion house known for its thin silk jersey pieces in splashy prints. A friend of mine who is a frequent international traveler also wears Leonard— the clothes weigh almost nothing and rarely wrinkle—so Easterling's choice seemed the perfect thing for what is presumably the ultimate trip. Then there was the champagne. Prior to her demise, Easterling drank a lot of it. She even carried around a little case of Waterford flutes because she didn't like imbibing her favorite Veuve Clicquot from inferior vessels. But it was generous of her to share. Veuve for a thousand is no small investment in something destined to go flat in your own glass.

And there was the food: fried eggplant, lump crabmeat in pastry shells, and fried oysters. Now, these happen to be some of the exact things I serve at most of my own parties—and a far cry from the funeral food we are used to in my part of the world (casseroles, weird layered salads, fried chicken, pound cake, tomato aspic). Funeral food is such an exhaustive culinary and cultural subject that Gayden Metcalfe, from my hometown of Greenville, Mississippi, devoted an entire book to the subject, called *Being Dead Is No Excuse*. In another book, by Michael Lee West, called *Consuming Passions: A Food-Obsessed Life*, the author includes a "Funeral Food" chapter in which she advises against fare like that served at Easterling's farewell: "I myself have never seen appetizers at a funeral."

Of course, Easterling's affair was not the usual post–church service groaning-board, but a cocktail party (or, in the words of her daughter, "a really nice way to say, 'The party's over'"). But I started thinking: If we plan everything else about the way we go out (hymns and readers, casket versus cremation), why not plan the menu? Even death-row inmates get to choose their last meal. Since for the rest of us the exact date for that particular repast is a tad harder to predict, we can do the next best thing by arranging for a swell meal for our mourners.

In her book, the skittish West also counsels against bringing desserts with names like Death by Chocolate, but if there's any occasion that calls for humor on a menu, it is this one. So with that in mind, I'll be serving the delicious champagne cocktail devised by Ernest Hemingway called Death in the Afternoon (an ounce of Pernod or absinthe at the bottom of a flute, topped with chilled champagne), though a Corpse Reviver No. 2 would not be out of place. There will also be a whole lot of tasty appetizers passed on trays, including my mother's to-die-for (sorry, couldn't resist) fried eggplant.

Judy's Fried Eggplant

SERVES 6 AS AN HORS D'OEUVRE

Ingredients

> 1 tbsp. salt
> 1 large eggplant, peeled and sliced crosswise into
>   quarter-inch slices
> 1 sleeve Ritz crackers (or more, as needed)
> 3 large eggs, beaten well
> Vegetable oil

Preparation

Fill a large bowl with ice water and add the salt. Stir to blend and add eggplant slices. Soak for about an hour. Meanwhile, crush the Ritz crackers by wrapping the sleeve in a dish towel and beating with a rolling pin. Or pulse a couple of times in a food processor. (You want them to have a bit of texture, like coarse bread crumbs, so do not pulverize them too finely.)

Drain the eggplant and dry carefully. Dip each slice in beaten egg to coat well and dredge in cracker crumbs, pressing to make sure they adhere. Transfer onto paper towels. Heat about two inches of oil over medium-high heat until very hot. (It should be around 375 degrees—if you don't have a thermometer, stick the handle of a wooden spoon into the oil. If the oil starts steadily bubbling around the handle, you are ready to go.) Fry the eggplant in batches (do not crowd pan) until golden brown, about a minute or two on each side. Add more oil as needed.

Drain on paper towels and sprinkle with salt.

Beyond the Butterball

ONE OF MY MORE MEMORABLE THANKSGIVING MIDDAY meals was eaten in my parents' kitchen, standing up. I'd cooked hamburgers for my father and me, and we ate them hanging over the counter because the juices from the meat had mingled (in an entirely delicious way) with the homemade mayo I'd spread on the toasted buns (actually English muffins) and were dripping (not unpleasantly) down our chins. It was memorable mainly because it did not involve turkey, or even turkey burgers, but also because the whole enterprise took less than fifteen minutes and did not require a single Pyrex dish. I should admit, here, that we'd been invited to a festive sit-down Thanksgiving dinner at someone else's house, which freed us up to invent our own lunch, so we didn't actually boycott the whole turkey-and-dressing-and-sweet-potato extravaganza. But I've thought more than once about how great it would be if, at least occasionally, on the fourth Thursday of November I could ditch the turkey altogether and give thanks that the pilgrims came to America so that the whole nation could later savor something as fine as a perfectly cooked burger on a bun (preferably accompanied by a nice red burgundy).

That kitchen lunch was an accident of sorts, but a couple of years ago I purposely veered off the well-trodden Turkey Day path, at least a little, at an outdoor Thanksgiving lunch on my former New Orleans lawn. Inspired by a piece I'd researched about the origins of the Pilgrims' first feast back in 1621, I decided to stage one based—very loosely, as it turns out—on their menu. This is not easy. The Plymouth settlers had no flour, very little sugar, and no potatoes. We know from a couple of surviving accounts that they did have five deer, given to them by the very nice Wampanoag Indians who also joined them at the table (this was clearly before our Native hosts knew what really, really bad guests—Thanksgiving or otherwise—future waves of settlers would turn out to be), the corn the Indians taught them to grow, and "the excellent seafish" that abounded in the nearby waters, including clams, cod, and lobster. The governor had sent a small party out "fowling" for the occasion, so there were ducks to be sure, but there is no evidence a turkey was actually served.

For our feast, we caved and had two turkeys, both wild and domestic, just in case, but we also grilled some oysters along with sausages made of both venison and duck. We put more oysters in the cornbread dressing and had another dressing made of shrimp and mirlitons, but then, you know, various guests insisted on bringing staples like yeast rolls and jellied cranberry sauce and sweet potatoes with the dread marshmallows on top and pies, including pumpkin, which I hate more than pretty much anything in the world. This is always a problem—at one point in the menu planning, no matter how inventive you try to get, Thanksgiving ends up being a forced march down the assorted memory lanes of way too many people. Fortunately, we had some more useful stuff the pilgrims didn't have, such as my friend Elizabeth's frozen Red Roosters (our very own Thanksgiving tradition composed of cranberry juice, orange juice, and vodka). Plus, we were dressed, nominally, in costume, which tends to lighten things up. I had on a full-blown Indian headdress, made of the lovely brown and white feathers from the underbelly of a peacock, and my friend Joan Griswold, the talented painter, whipped up an entire black-and-white pilgrim's getup with her trusty sewing machine. Her husband, the writer and humorist Roy Blount, Jr., looked extremely fetching in a headpiece he made by tying a fake cornucopia found at the grocery store to an ancient Saints visor with scruffy artificial white hair on the top.

I love a theme, and I like turkey just fine. But you do have to wonder why the pilgrims' immediate descendants didn't pick up on the yummy lobster aspect of the proceedings, say, or at least the duck. (I once served Scott Peacock's duck stuffed with red rice and oyster dressing, which seems to me a slightly more realistic homage.) I also started wondering what would have happened if the first settlers had landed somewhere else. If they'd somehow made it up the mouth of the Mississippi to the Delta, where I was born, for example, we might well be eating bear on our national holiday. Well into the nineteenth century, the still sparsely inhabited Delta was so chock-full of the furry creatures that the famed African-American hunting guide Holt Collier was said to have shot three thousand alone. Collier served as Theodore Roosevelt's guide when the president came for the hunt of 1902—a now famous trip that resulted in the "teddy bear." Roosevelt was on a lunch break and unable to take the shot when Collier ran the bear across the clearing. So to protect his dogs the guide was forced to tie the bear to a tree. When the president returned, he refused to shoot the tethered animal, an act that was later captured in a cartoon, which in turn led to the stuffed toy. Determined to get a legitimate bear, Roosevelt came back five years later, a trip that resulted (according to Collier's biographer, Minor Buchanan) in "three bears, six deer, one wild turkey, twelve squirrels, one duck, one opossum, and one wildcat." The party ate everything but the wildcat, and I guess we should all be grateful that the pilgrims didn't manage to run across a possum or some squirrels.

Bears are currently endangered in Mississippi but they still find their way to the Delta. Last spring when the river was in flood stage a rather large specimen was found up a tree in downtown Greenville. I've not had the pleasure of dining on one, but apparently they were once a sought-after food source. In a piece he wrote on bear hunting for *Delta Magazine*, my friend Hank Burdine reported that Collier got twenty-three dollars for a dressed deer, but up to sixty dollars for a bear. His clientele primarily consisted of men in frontier camps who'd turned up to build the levees or railroads or both, but plenty of other folks were on the bears' trail. After a Confederate colonel named Robert Bobo rebuilt his farm near Clarksdale, he still managed to spend most of his time in the swamps, where during a three-month period in 1887 he reported killing 304 bears, 54 deer, and 9 panthers. Burdine cites a journal written by Bobo's daughter-in-law in which she recalls the "festive mood in their setting out for the wild country, with the string of four-mule wagons, the dozens of dogs racing here and there, and the hunters themselves, mounted on their fine-spirited horses. The men were gone for weeks and lived on bear steaks and stew."

The meat itself, she says, was "quite coarse and tough, but good." I'm not convinced, but either way, that expedition sounds like a hell of a lot more fun than the exploits of the long-suffering pilgrims. But then they were not a people known for their fun-loving ways or for their way around a kitchen either, even when they had a bit more to work with. In David Hackett Fischer's *Albion's Seed*, a terrific account of the folkways of four groups that came over from England, he writes: "Among both high-born and humble folk, eating was a more sensual experience in Virginia than in Massachusetts. There was nothing in the Chesapeake colonies to equal the relentless austerity of New England's 'canonical dish' of cold baked beans." No kidding. By that time (the eighteenth century), we were busy munching on far more lavish renditions of that first Thanksgiving fowl. Recipes from the era include one for a duck fricassee made with pickled oysters, a bottle of claret, copious amounts of butter and egg yolks, and a quarter pound of bacon. I might well make that this year. Or maybe some dark venison chili followed by a big plate of fried catfish and hush puppies. We should be most thankful for the bounty just outside our door, after all, and when Roosevelt made yet another visit to Mississippi, in 1911, the local folks were smart enough to know that. The luncheon in honor of the former president kicked off with mint juleps and included okra gumbo with beaten biscuits, deviled crab, and "Fried Milk Fed Chicken, Southern Style" with grilled sweet potatoes.

Man. Mint juleps and fried chicken. That's a Thanksgiving menu that might distract even the most devout turkey diehards.

Recipe for Longevity

FOR THE LAST EIGHT WEEKS I'VE RECEIVED AN EMAIL with the subject line "What's your address? (sending you a cookbook) . . ." from an outfit called Paleo Reboot. Every day, I dutifully unsubscribe, report the message as spam, and delete, and every day I get another one. (I realize I could avoid many such irritating missives by getting rid of my AOL account, but old habits die hard and I've decided it's cool rather than lazy to be a holdout.) I have no intention of sending these people my home address, but I finally did take a look at the website, where I discovered a young man named Dr. Ryan Lazarus (not an MD, exactly, but rather a "certified practitioner of functional medicine and Doctor of Chiropractic"), who was touting books related to the phenomenon that is the Paleo diet.

For those of you who have been living under a rock—or who long ago abandoned AOL—the Paleo diet is a high-protein, high-fiber eating plan that purports to mimic the habits of our ancestral hunter-gatherers by eliminating dairy, refined sugar, legumes, cereal, grains, potatoes, and beef from cows that have dined on anything but grass. The premise (and promise) is that making like a caveman will enable you to get lean and all but eliminate the risk of heart disease and diabetes, along with a whole host of other ills. There has been much back-and-forth about the pros and cons of such a diet, with one of the biggest cons (yep, that's a pun) being that no one could possibly know what the real Paleo diet actually consisted of and that different groups ate different stuff. Aboriginal Australians dined primarily on animal products, for example, while the Kitavans of Papua New Guinea ate fish and coconuts. Also, not only have our genes changed more in the last ten thousand years than Paleo proponents would have us believe, but also so have the species of fish and fruit, etc., that early man ate. Whatever. I'll try anything for a week or two, but I have no intention of living a life devoid of—just to name a few—rice and gravy, lady peas, butter beans, biscuits, ice cream, yeast rolls, steak frites, or cheese.

Instead, when it comes to ancestors, I prefer to draw on the eating habits of my more recent—rather more evolved—ones, including my paternal great-grandfather Sterling Price Reynolds, who died at age 106, and my three great-aunts who lived well into their nineties. My father grew up in the home of Mr. Reynolds (as he was mostly called, even by his best friend and brother-in-law, Uncle Gideon Crews), a sprawling place near the banks of the Mississippi River in Caruthersville, Missouri, that housed three generations of family. Even though Daddy recently turned eighty-eight himself, he can still recall, with vivid accuracy and enthusiasm, the three daily meals taken at his grandfather's table. "Doctor" Lazarus, as well as Loren Cordain, the Ph.D. and professor emeritus who is the self-declared "founder of the Paleo Diet Movement," would be appalled by every one of them.

Right off the bat, breakfast, which was always served at 7:00 A.M. sharp, was full of Paleo no-nos. There was fruit (acceptable), but it was invariably topped off with the cream left over from the daily churning of butter, as was the oatmeal (unacceptable). To add to these sins, there were eggs (acceptable), but they were fried in the aforementioned butter and accompanied by cured ham (there was a smokehouse) and bacon or both (Cordain recommends uncured pork chops instead). The noon lunch was even worse: chicken and dumplings, fried catfish, or a roast of red meat carved at table, except on Sundays, when there was usually fried chicken; spoon bread or fried hot-water cornbread (slathered with butter); greens and/or field peas cooked with cured ham hocks, plus all the vegetables in season from the garden. Dinner, at six, was a slightly more formal affair. There would be beefsteak or quail, all manner of potatoes, plus yeast rolls and biscuits and sometimes popovers too. Paleo-friendly additions included oysters off the overnight train from New Orleans, fresh spinach or asparagus from the bed, watermelon every night in summer, and ambrosia for dessert—but even the ambrosia got doused with cream.

The beverages would also have been highly alien to *Homo habilis*. Hot coffee was served during breakfast, iced tea (albeit unsweetened) during lunch and dinner, with more hot coffee served afterward. Before dinner the grown-ups enjoyed a highball (or two or three) of bourbon. This often took the form of an old-fashioned, which I'm pretty sure was made with regular old refined sugar as opposed to the coconut syrup used in the version posted on paleococktails.com. While the good professor Cordain is opposed to caffeine and frowns on distilled spirits and wine with sulfites (which is pretty much all of them), he graciously allows his non-obese followers to cheat 15 percent of the time.

Mr. Reynolds didn't smoke, but his daughter, my grandmother, was a lifelong smoker, as was her husband and his sisters, the long-lived great-aunts. (We'll never know how long my grandparents would have hung around—they were in their eighties and as healthy as horses when they were killed in a car crash.) I was especially close to my aunt Margaret, who celebrated her ninetieth birthday at a big bash, where she was photographed with her "little" sisters Helen and Jessie (both in their late eighties) sitting side by side on a sofa. Each woman is holding a highball and a cigarette, with their cigarette "purses," those old-fashioned snap-top things with side pockets for lighters, positioned prominently in their laps. I never saw Aunt Margaret without hers, and as a child I was forever entertained by that popping sound her lips made against the filter as she wrenched the last possible drag out of her Benson & Hedges 100.

Now, let me hasten to add that I'm not for one minute advocating smoking—I know way too many people not nearly as lucky as the aunts. I'm just saying (and hoping like hell) that a lot of this is luck of the gene-pool draw. (And in Aunt Margaret's case, the bourbon and tobacco might very well have been offset by the fact that she never married or had children—she was an extraordinarily cheerful human.) But I do think we *Homo sapiens* could be okay with a slightly longer view than that taken by Professor Cordain. His list of non-Paleo foods that adversely affect the health of humanity includes but is not remotely limited to potato chips, tacos, hamburgers, french fries, doughnuts, chips and salsa, sandwiches, sausage, pancakes, and pizza—in short, "just about any other product man/woman has their hand in producing." At this rate, we'll be picking blueberries off bushes with our teeth.

Cordain clearly has a tiny tendency toward the pompous, so I'll just respond by noting that I am profoundly grateful to the "man/woman" who figured out pretty early on that the noble pig would taste mighty damn delicious if you took your hands and salted and cured various cuts of him, notably his belly and his haunch. Bacon and country ham are, as noted, on Cordain's list of stuff that is adverse to our health, but in this he is not alone. A year ago, the International Agency for Research on Cancer (IARC), a World Health Organization group, announced its findings that the consumption of processed meat (anything "transformed through salting, curing, fermentation, smoking, or other processes to enhance flavour or improve preservation") causes cancer, and the consumption of red meat "probably" does.

Not surprisingly, the North American Meat Institute posted a host of studies that found differently. There was even a series of YouTube videos featuring the senior vice president for public affairs calmly telling viewers that "it is IARC's job to find cancer hazards," and that so far the outfit has found "sunlight, breathing air . . . working in a barbershop" all to be causes of the disease. Both camps have a point. If you bake yourself in the sun, you might get skin cancer and die. But my great-grandfather had a daily serving of cured and red meats (and alcohol), and he led the parade, on foot, that marked his one hundredth birthday.

Though there was a lot of hoopla when the study came out, it seems unlikely that my fellow bacon lovers are going to give it up anytime soon. Americans eat an average of eighteen pounds of bacon a year, each. If you remove the vegetarians, vegans, and some Paleo dieters from the list, that means many of us are eating a highly disproportionate share of the roughly 5,760,000,000 pounds of pork strips consumed across the country each year. And that's not even counting the Canadians. In a recent poll, 43 percent of our brothers and sisters to the north said they preferred bacon to sex.

Also, it turns out that bacon has some health benefits of a sort. A study at the International Centre for Life at Newcastle University in England examined why the classic English bacon sandwich (a "bacon butty") was a near perfect treat to cure a hangover. The researcher Elin Roberts told the *Telegraph*, "Bread doesn't soak up alcohol but is high in carbohydrates that boost blood-sugar levels and speed up the metabolism, helping to get rid of alcohol quickly. Bingeing on alcohol depletes brain neuro-transmitters but bacon, which is rich in protein, contains amino acids that top these up, giving you a clearer head."

Gwyneth Paltrow would most likely say it's all about finding your balance, but I'd bet big money that the whole time she lived in London with Chris Martin, she never ate a bacon butty. Me, I'm gonna take my chances. One of the world's great pleasures is a dry martini, up, before moving along to a perfectly cooked steak and a bottle of a fairly big red. And then there is the trifecta of Paleo contraband, the pimento cheese dog at Atlanta's Varsity. Bread/cheese/dog equals a Paleo nightmare, but for many of us, it's heaven in a bite. Sadly, our more distant ancestors, who lived, at most, to the ripe old age of forty, never had the pleasure.

Make Mine a Scotch

IN 1975, WALKER PERCY WROTE A NOW FAMOUS ESSAY FOR *Esquire* called, simply, "Bourbon." This was long before the stuff became a cult and a bottle of twenty-three-year-old Pappy could set you back more than two thousand dollars. In the piece, Percy confesses up front that he's no connoisseur (his preferred brand was Early Times, and he was no stranger to the rather rougher satisfactions of long-ago labels like Two Natural); his subject lay in "the aesthetic of bourbon drinking" and the "pleasure of knocking [it] back." I will have to take his word for it. I don't like bourbon.

Let me say up front that I do like Walker Percy. You will not find a bigger fan than me. I reread *The Last Gentleman* every year and *Lancelot* and *Love in the Ruins* almost as much. I reread the bourbon essay too, quite a bit, because like so much of what Percy wrote, it makes me sit up and say, "Yes, yes, I know that!" It also makes me laugh out loud. To (very loosely) paraphrase

Percy, there are few better defenses against the anomie of the twenty-first century than the shock of recognition and a good chuckle.

But for me Scotch whiskey is the far superior front line. In *Love in the Ruins*, set in "a time near the end of the world," the protagonist holes up in an abandoned Howard Johnson's with fifteen cases of Early Times and a whole lot of Vienna sausage. By contrast, I could face down pretty much anything with some Dewar's and Campbell's chicken noodle. I do not for one minute begrudge Percy his bourbon. And while it doesn't have the same effect on me, I totally get his description of "the little explosion of Kentucky U.S.A. sunshine in the cavity of the nasopharynx and the hot bosky bite of Tennessee summertime" whenever he throws back a shot. That is great stuff on the page. But then—and here is where I have one tiny, tiny quibble with my hero—he gets a tad judgmental about my own whiskey of choice (which, by the way, is the world's most popular spirit). He says he finds drinking Scotch to be "like looking at a picture of Noel Coward." That's a great line too, and very funny, but I happen to adore Noel Coward. There's also this: "The [Scotch] whiskey assaults the nasopharynx with all the excitement of paregoric." Unlike Percy, I am not a doctor and I don't know much about my nasopharynx, but I do know that when I drink Scotch, there's a warmth surging through my veins that makes me feel immediately better about what Percy aptly described as "the sadness of the old dying Western world" and enables me to be far more compassionate toward my fellow man. The feeling I get sounds not all that unlike the description junkies give of that first lovely hit, which is one of the many reasons I've never tried heroin.

Percy's barbs aside, being a Scotch drinker from the Deep South has been something of a cross to bear my whole life. One of the many stereotypes we Southerners have long had to put up with is that all of us are unreconstructed devotees of corn liquor. People are forever offering me glasses of bourbon— and in far too many instances, handing me a highball before I can put them off. Single-malt Scotch may be as hip these days as small-batch bourbon among the sort of people who keep up with such things, but there are lots of places down here where even a simple bottle of J&B is not easy to come by. Take, for example, the Grey Goose, a now (extremely sadly) defunct bar in Delcambre, Louisiana. My first visit there was on one of life's seriously perfect nights. My then beloved and I had driven west from New Orleans to eat crawfish at Black's in Abbeville and generally get up to no good.

When we passed the Goose, an old roadhouse on the two-lane highway between Abbeville and New Iberia, we could hear Patsy Cline's "Crazy" streaming out the open windows, so, naturally, we pulled into the oyster-shell lot. The crowd mostly consisted of drunk shrimpers, just off the boat and still in their white rubber boots, and the proprietor, a woman with an almost incomprehensible Cajun accent and a slight beard, managed to make me understand that she had not washed her face since the former governor Edwin Edwards had kissed her during his last reelection campaign, which at that point would have been eight years earlier. There was a large photo of Edwards on the wall and some aquatic taxidermy, I think, and when I asked the bartender for a Scotch and water, he just looked at me, utterly uncomprehending. Looking back, I'm sure it was the first time the poor man had heard the word *Scotch*, much less received an order for it, and I cannot imagine why I placed it, but he got down on the floor and rifled through the lower cabinet, arising triumphantly with a dusty bottle of VO, which I declined in favor of a cold Bud—delicious but not the same. Now I make like my mother, who never travels without a giant plastic flask of Dewar's or Johnny Walker Black. Twenty-first-century anomie is no small thing to reckon with, and one doesn't want to be caught off guard.

The brand of Scotch I grew up drinking was called John Handy (presumably named after the Scot who graced the bottle in tartans and a tam). I developed a pretty healthy taste for it at a relatively young age by enthusiastically clearing up the glasses during my parents' frequent and lively cocktail parties, and I kept at it until they stopped making it in the early 2000s. Though Mississippi was dry in my youth (it was the last state to repeal the Eighteenth Amendment, in 1966), booze flowed freely—it just meant that we were dependent on the brands the bootlegger stocked. I know our own personal bootlegger carried Old Crow bourbon because my mother left a bottle in the mailbox at Christmas as a present for the postman. My father recalls that Ballantine's and Grand Old Parr were among the Scotch offerings. The latter, featuring an etching of a bearded man on a fake parchment label and cobwebs etched into the glass, was a big favorite, especially with his lady friends (before my mother's time), who liked using the empty bottle as a candleholder. When, on Daddy's first trip to Westminster Abbey, he encountered Thomas Parr's grave, the guide told him Parr was famous only for being very old. The label did not lie.

Daddy and his friends switched to John Handy after it was served at a party given by the local bon vivant Larry Pryor, who was a world traveler and renowned foxhunt host (I learned to ride on a horse named Squire Pryor), a bachelor who generally served the best of everything so everybody figured that was the way to go. It turned out to be imported to New Orleans, where it was mixed with the local tap water and bottled before being distributed by the Schwegmann's grocery store chain. It wasn't until I went off to boarding school that I learned that John Handy wasn't exactly the toast of the nation. In an attempt to seem older than my sixteen years, I asked for it by name in the D.C. liquor store where my friends and I occasionally scored. The man at the counter happened to be from Louisiana, and he not only refused to sell us anything, he also advised me not to embarrass myself further by asking for a bottle that no one in our nation's capital would likely have ever seen.

My father and his business partner Barthell Joseph remained staunch Handy defenders until its demise (I am betting that its seven-dollars-a-fifth price tag had a whole lot to do with their loyalty, but they also really liked it—the last present I got from Barthell before he died was two cases of half gallons, for which I was grateful). But my mother made the switch to Dewar's years ago. I recently sampled the half gallon I keep stashed in Barthell's memory, and I now understand why, though I owe the good Mr. Handy a lot for nurturing my love of a whiskey that saw me through many trying times and even more delightful ones.

There was one other thing in the Percy essay that bugged me. He said he thought of Scotch drinkers "as upwardly mobile Americans, Houston and New Orleans businessmen who graduate from bourbon about the same time they shed seersucker for Lilly slacks." Ouch. I know a lot of people in Houston and New

Orleans, but most of them aren't exactly businessmen in the strict sense of the term, so I asked my good friend Will Feltus, who does this sort of thing for a living, to tell me who exactly does drink Scotch. A bourbon drinker from Natchez, Will had just finished studying a Nielsen Scarborough 2016 survey of two hundred thousand booze consumers, and the first fact he delivered was a shocker: A whopping 61 percent of the respondents (American adults over eighteen) reported not drinking *any* distilled spirits in the last thirty days. My first thought was that we people in Mississippi did not endure (the admittedly not very hard) hardship of living in a dry state so that other people would not engage in their God-given right to drink freely, without any encumbrances or inhibitions. The second was that no wonder this country of ours is so messed up—how the hell else are you supposed to keep Percy's noxious particles and the general trauma of everyday existence at bay without the odd nip?

Of those who did imbibe, it turns out that Scotch drinkers are not "upwardly mobile" but more "upscale," full stop—better educated and more likely to have an AmEx card. They are also way more male than female, tend toward the middle politically (bourbon drinkers are further to the right), and mostly live and drink in the mid-Atlantic and Pacific states. The rest of the info is as you would predict. Bourbon remains more popular in the South (especially Kentucky, Tennessee, Mississippi, and Arkansas) than anywhere else, but not by all that wide a margin, maybe because all the women are drinking vodka. There was also the finding that 42 percent of Scotch drinkers will also drink bourbon but only 20 percent of bourbon drinkers will drink Scotch. This bears out what I've always liked to think: that we Scotch drinkers as a class are more open-minded, more diverse and willing in our appetites—equally at home listening to, say, Noel Coward's "I Went to a Marvellous Party" or the Kentucky-born Loretta Lynn singing "Don't Come Home a Drinkin' (with Lovin' on Your Mind)." It's certainly true that these days I would not turn down a swig of Pappy or even a modest glass of straight-up Blanton's, but I'll remain ever true to the amber elixir that warms both my blood and my heart. And I'm in good company. When the young Winston Churchill covered the Second Boer War as a correspondent for the *Morning Post*, he took along roughly $4,000 worth of wine and spirits, including eighteen bottles of St.-Emilion and another eighteen of ten-year-old Scotch.

Stone-Ground Killer

EVERYBODY KNOWS THAT FOOD—OR, MORE TO THE point, its consumption—can kill you, especially if you happen to live in the South. Seven of the ten states with the nation's highest adult obesity rates are below the Mason-Dixon Line, usually led, alas, by my own home state of Mississippi. (I swear, at this point our license plates should just sport the motto "First in fatness, last in literacy".) Not surprisingly, most of those same states have the country's highest premature death rates. Leaving aside the slightly more complicated issues of violent crime and poverty that also factor in, we are really adept at eating ourselves to death.

It's not always our fault. I covered Bill Clinton's reelection campaign in 1996 and over a period of about six very long months, I listened to at least a hundred speeches in which he pledged to make the country safe from E. coli, the sinister bacterium that can lurk in raw vegetables and undercooked beef.

In this post-9/11 era of al-Qaeda, ISIS, and God knows what else, that actually seems sort of sweet, but it's a real deal. Despite the former president's best efforts, thousands of people still get sick and some even die each year from E. coli. And then of course there are botulism and salmonella. In April, the Centers for Disease Control and Prevention, which keeps track of this stuff, reported the largest botulism outbreak in forty years when twenty-five people were stricken at a church potluck in Ohio. The cause: a tub of homemade potato salad. Five years earlier, more than two dozen people came down with salmonella poisoning after dining on rattlesnake cakes at a restaurant called The Fort in Morrison, Colorado, but it seems to me they were asking for it.

Scary as all that sounds, the subject at hand is not food contamination or even consumption; it is food, specifically grits, as deadly weapon. This past summer, for example, a Maryland woman was charged with second-degree assault for pouring hot grits on a man as he slept and then beating him with a baseball bat. To me, this raises the question of what exactly constitutes first-degree assault, but I digress. The incident was not the first time someone used grits to settle a score. Last year, a Florida man named Edward Holley was charged with attempted murder after dousing a man with grits, covering 30 percent of his body with second- and third-degree burns. Apparently a dispute had taken place the night before, so when Holley saw the victim on his front porch the next morning, he told police he simply grabbed the nearest weapon, "a pan of grease and grits" cooking on his stove.

It turns out that grits attacks are something of an established trend. In Louisiana, especially, folks seem to always have a batch simmering at the ready. A year before the unrepentant Holley attacked his neighbor (he allegedly told police, "If you're going to arrest me, then just arrest me now, 'cause next time I am going to kill him"), a New Orleans man was convicted of aggravated second-degree battery after he poured boiling grits on his wife and beat her with the pot for good measure. Three years before that, a woman in nearby Boutte was arrested for pouring what police described as a "huge pot" of hot grits on her boyfriend while he slept. In an especially ill-timed move, he'd made the mistake of telling her he wanted to break up before repairing to bed.

To be fair, grits are not the only food or food-related weapon in the food pantry arsenal. When I first started spending time in Louisiana in the early 1990s, I heard tales of irate wives scalding their husbands with boiling red beans laced with lye. The citizens of Florida are apparently more partial to beef. In 2009, police arrested a Central Florida woman for beating her disabled boyfriend in the head with a raw rib-eye steak after he requested a dinner roll rather than the slice of bread she had served him. Just a few days earlier, in Port St. Lucie, a man was arrested for shoving a hamburger in his girlfriend's face at a restaurant called Dick's. Food can also be involved in slightly less direct but no less lethal ways. In Cleveland, Ohio, an over-weight woman killed her boyfriend by sitting on him while he was facedown on the sofa.

Still, you can't beat grits for access, convenience, and hot and sticky effectiveness. The most famous grits attack, which occurred in 1974, involved the great soul singer Al Green. Green was brushing his teeth in his Memphis bathroom when a jealous female fan, whom he had unwisely invited to his house, poured a pot of boiling grits down his back, causing third-degree burns and months of hospitalization. Though Green likes to put distance between that harrowing incident and his becoming an ordained Baptist minister two years later, I can't believe there's no correlation. Either way, Green is still as soulful as ever and his mostly musical services at the Full Gospel Tabernacle in Memphis are not to be missed. The attack on the singer also proved inspirational to his colleagues. Usher made use of the grits incident in "Truth Hurts," and in "Everything," Method Man raps, "Trust me, I'm hot as they get, like Al Green getting hit by a pot of them grits."

The proliferation of assaults by grits gives a whole new meaning to the term *packing heat* (not to mention *white-hot*), but there's more than one irony here. First of all, the great majority of grits sold in America are made by Quaker Oats, which as early as 1877 registered as its trademark with the U.S. Patent Office "a figure of a man in 'Quaker garb.'" Quakers, otherwise known as members of the Religious Society of Friends, are a famously nonviolent group—though it must be said that wielding some grits is one way to get around their refusal to bear arms. Also, it turns out that the actual consumption of grits is good for you. Not only are they usually gluten-free, but they also have fewer fat grams than oatmeal.

It comes as no surprise that grits have been co-opted by those with violent intent. They've always been enormously versatile. The best cheese grits dish I ever made was the result of dumping leftover odds and ends from a cheese platter, including a creamy Cashel blue, into a simmering pot of them along with a generous pinch of cayenne. This was at the very late end of a raucous evening when everyone needed a bit of a blotter for the booze (another healthy and excellent use of grits). So with that in mind, and in an attempt to restore the reputation of the humble grit as something good for the body and the soul, I offer up this recipe for grits cakes. They're terrific as a base for pretty much anything from duck étouffée and sautéed shrimp to a chunky tomato sauce, and they are a tasty replacement for English muffins in eggs Benedict or Sardou. The versions on the menu at the Manhattan restaurant Maysville come topped with a dab of bourbon mayonnaise and slivers of country ham and are so heavenly they might even tempt the understandably grits-shy Reverend Green.

Grits Cakes

MAKES ABOUT 10 SMALL CAKES

Ingredients

> 2 cups milk
> 2 cups water
> 1 tsp. salt
> 2 tbsp. butter
> 1 cup stone-ground grits
> ½ cup grated sharp cheddar
> ¼ cup Parmesan cheese
> Pinch cayenne pepper
> Vegetable or other flavorless oil
> Flour

Preparation

In a saucepan, bring the milk and water to a boil; add the salt and butter. Whisk in grits and reduce heat to a simmer. Cook, stirring occasionally, until grits are done. (This should take at least 30 minutes, depending on the grits.) Remove from heat and stir in cheeses and cayenne.

Oil a shallow 9-inch baking pan and pour in grits, spreading evenly with a spatula. (The grits should be about 1 inch thick, or a little less.) Cover with plastic wrap and refrigerate until firm. Cut in squares or triangles, or use a 2½- to 3-inch biscuit cutter to make rounds. Dredge lightly in flour.

Pour ½ inch of oil into a large nonstick skillet set over medium-high heat. Add the grits cakes and fry until golden and crispy, about 2 or 3 minutes on each side.

Drain on paper towels.

Part Four

The South in All Its Glory— Or Not

The South by the Numbers

In 2011, *PARADE* MAGAZINE PUT OUT AN ISSUE WITH A cover story called "America by the Numbers: Fun Facts from the 50 States." Once again, the South was shunned. We were glaringly absent from the top rankings in the Physical Activity, High School Graduation Rates, and Recent Dental Visits categories. None of our cities was voted best for online dating or bike culture; we are not the most vegetarian friendly nor do we eat the most fruits and veggies (Vermont, not surprisingly, took that honor). We don't give the most to charity and we don't get the most sun. Shockingly, we do not even have the most strip clubs, but Richmond did come in at number three among the most tattooed cities. The South was hardly mentioned in the rest of the article except for the Sleepiest States category (West Virginia, Tennessee, Kentucky, and Florida ranked one, two, three, and five, respectively) and the Cosmetic Surgery category. But even that was weird. The South Atlantic states get the most buttock implants, while South Central states go for the most hair transplants.

To recap: According to the portrait painted by *Parade*'s "Fun Facts," we are a region of sleepy, tattooed, but slightly vain people who try to cover up our baldness and want bigger butts. Okay, they didn't come out and say it quite that way, but I found myself wishing they had dug a little harder to come up with a few more fun facts for us. They could have said, for example, that we have the most state dogs and the most state horses. Everybody can claim a state flower and a state bird, but only twelve states have official horses and eleven have dogs, and ours are unquestionably the prettiest.

In Louisiana, there's the noble Catahoula leopard dog, for example, who not only can have gorgeous white-blue eyes but is also tough enough to catch and pen wild cattle and hogs. By contrast, the Massachusetts dog, the Boston terrier, has cute ears but is pretty much good for nothing. All our dogs do stuff. Texas's beautiful and highly intelligent Blue Lacy, which originated in the state, can herd livestock, tree game, and run traplines, while South Carolina's adorable Boykin spaniel is an excellent small hunting dog with the added benefit of not rocking the boat while on the water. Likewise, Virginia has the American foxhound, Maryland has the Chesapeake Bay retriever, North Carolina has the Plott hound, and if the state legislature would get off its collective ass and finally vote on the thing, Georgia would have the ever lovable and highly useful golden retriever. Finally, we have the really cool distinction of having the only two state bats in the country, the Virginia big-eared bat and Texas's Mexican free-tailed bat.

Now, those are the kinds of state stats I can get behind, but it must be said that a lot of our facts are not so fun—and certainly not by *Parade*'s wholesome standards. We have the most violent crime, the most guns, and the most shooting deaths. We have by far the lowest health rankings, which translates into the most heart attacks and cases of diabetes, the highest cholesterol, and a whole bunch of smokers (Kentucky smokes the most, with Mississippi not far behind). We have the least amount of binge drinking, which would be good news, except that there are no statistics that I could find for people who drink pretty much all the time.

We are also the fattest people in America—Mississippi is the most obese state, followed by Louisiana, Tennessee, and Kentucky. (Which begs the question: If we are already so damn hefty, what are we doing getting all those butt implants? Trying to keep up with the Joneses?) Not surprisingly, Vermonters, who chomp on all that healthy roughage, are among the skinniest, along with folks from Connecticut, Massachusetts, Hawaii, and Colorado.

Parade got its fruit and vegetable consumption info from an outfit called America's Health Rankings, but its research is sorely lacking in interesting facts like, say, who eats the most spaghetti and meatballs or who drinks the most Dr Pepper. I mean, I can make a pretty safe bet that we eat the most grits, the most barbecue, the most red beans and rice, the most boudin and andouille, the most perloos and pilaus, the most gumbo . . . I could go on. I tried really hard to find out who ate the most pork rinds, and I'm pretty sure we do, but we have some stiff competition from Ohio, where there is an annual festival and at least three producers. But what we do have are the only religious pork rinds.

One of the many significant facts about us that *Parade* left out is that we go to church with way, way more frequency than anybody else. (Vermont is in the bottom ten on church attendance, so we'll see how far all those leafy greens get them.) Anyway, an ingenious—or, more likely, just extremely pious—pork rind outfit in Tennessee has combined our love of the mighty rind with our love of the Lord. Bartlett-based Brimhall Foods makes a number of pork products, including Brim's Pork Fatback Cracklin Strips, which are described as "fried-out pork with attached skin." On their bags there is always a Bible verse, usually from John, so that it is possible to be munching on some pure pork while also being reassured that "God is light and in Him is not darkness at all." The rinds from Ohio, let me just make clear, do not come with such added consolation.

I have also never read of a case in Ohio—or anywhere else outside the South, for that matter—that involved bribery with pork rinds, which is another piece of evidence supporting my theory that we eat them more than anybody else. (If we didn't like them so much they wouldn't be successful bribe material. In fact, a lot of our more notable foodstuffs will do the trick—I once got out of a speeding ticket in Beulah, Mississippi, by bringing the justice of the peace a pecan pie from Sherman's in Greenville.)

Anyway, recently, in the town of Appalachia, Virginia, a small coal-mining town just miles from the Kentucky border, Mayor Ben Cooper and thirteen others were charged in a scheme that included buying votes with cigarettes, beer, and pork rinds. One of the cops booked with Cooper was also charged with pilfering prescription drugs and two guns from the evidence room, as well as recklessly handling a firearm when he used one of the guns to shoot himself in the leg at headquarters.

Festive stories like these have got me thinking that if *Parade* made just a tiny shift in its attitude and general outlook, those Fun Facts cover stories could be a lot more entertaining—and still very informative. They would also be far more inclusive of our region. By using the Appalachia case alone, the magazine could have had a nice little package handily illustrating the South's penchant for pork rinds, cigarettes, beer, and firearms, and if the pork rinds happened to be Brim's, religion would have made the mix as well.

Going Deep in Dixie

In January 2012, I read an article in the *Wall Street Journal* about a change in strategy at the St. Joe Company, the former timber and railroad outfit that's one of Florida's largest landowners. After the success of Seaside, the award-winning New Urbanist community founded in 1981 on the northwest Florida coast, St. Joe began working on its own master-planned developments, one of which, WaterColor, abuts Seaside and the other of which, WaterSound, is just down the road. Like pretty much everybody else in the luxury real estate business, St. Joe got slammed in the housing bust, and its new board of directors signaled to the SEC that it would be significantly reducing expenditures in the planned communities, which was the peg of the piece. Since I already knew that, I was about to turn the page when the last line of the story, written by a fellow named Robbie Whelan, caught my eye. The "area," he wrote, "is often derided for its deep southern feel and muggy climate."

Now, as it happens, I have spent a large part of my life in this particular "area," also known as the Panhandle. In fact, when I read the article, I was sitting in the living room of the house in Seaside my mother has owned for the past fifteen years. She'd spent much of her own childhood in an entirely different Florida, vacationing with her parents and grandparents in Palm Beach at the Breakers hotel. The "feel" there, as at so many of the other über-social, high-WASP (or at least formerly high-WASP) resorts along Florida's South Atlantic coast, is not so much regional—Deep South or otherwise—as tribal. The Palm Beach Breakers is not all that different in look and provenance from the Newport Breakers (a lot of Mr. Vanderbilt's summer houseguests in Rhode Island were also winter guests at Mr. Flagler's hotel), or, for that matter, from the *Andrea Doria*, the cruise ship on which my grandparents also vacationed before it sank.

My mother hated the Breakers. She and her nurse had to dress up just to cross the lobby to the pool; she spent her afternoons playing shuffleboard with my great-grandfather. There's a picture of him there, with my great-grandmother and my grandmother and some close family friends. The men are in tropical-weight suits with ties and pocket squares; my grandmother has on a printed silk day dress, white pumps, and a fair amount of diamonds and pearls. No one is smiling.

So it was that my own family spent vacations in Destin at the Frangista Beach motel. With her marriage to my father, my mother had already made one revolutionary move, from the plush confines of Nashville's Belle Meade to the swampy wilds of the Mississippi Delta; the leap from Palm Beach to the Panhandle was sort of the same thing. At the Frangista, the screen doors of the linoleum-tiled "suites" opened directly onto the beach, we rarely wore anything other than bathing suits, and there was certainly no shuffleboard. Instead, there was a next-door RV park, temporary home of one of my earliest crushes, a guy named Larry who caught rays atop his Winnebago and whose straw cowboy hat featured a band made of Pabst Blue Ribbon pull tabs, which were in ample supply.

My brothers and I and all our friends fished and swam and made ourselves peanut butter and jelly sandwiches for lunch, and at night we went with our parents to restaurants like the Sand Flea or the Blue Room for pompano and stuffed flounder. The grown people stayed up late drinking whiskey they bought at the Green Knight, a package store named for the garishly painted figure out front, while we went crabbing with the help of flashlights and the beach-loving dog Dexter, who belonged to my father's best friend, Nick. I'm sure that by the time July and August rolled around it was, in fact, plenty "muggy," but we didn't notice. That was what the water, and the ever-rumbling Frangista window units, were for.

It was easy and it was fun and I guess I'd been visiting for at least fifteen years when I discovered another photo of my grandmother at the beach, this time at a friend's vacation house on the bay near Destin, a place I never knew she'd been to. She has on capri pants (then better known as clam diggers), a sleeveless blouse, and no shoes. She doesn't know the photo is being taken, and she's leaning forward on her toes laughing, with what appears to be an actual can of beer in her hand. The photo astonished me for a great many reasons, not least because in all the years I knew her I had never seen my grandmother refresh herself with anything other than Beefeater's in a Baccarat glass, or shed her shoes in public for any reason other than to have someone paint Revlon's Windsor on her toenails.

Maybe that "deep southern" pull was strong enough to get my grandmother, a woman who once took my cousin and me trout fishing in exactly the same getup she had on in the photo from the Breakers, to shed her shoes. Whatever—I was just so relieved to learn that at least once she'd had some fun in the sun. The rest of us are still at it, though when Destin got a tad too overrun with high-rise condos, we moved our base of operations about twenty miles southeast to Seaside, which brings me back to the article.

First, let's get past the fact that the writer seems to imply that the same fate that's befallen pretty much every luxury real estate developer in the entire country happened to St. Joe because its land happened to be in a place that's hot and feels like the Deep South, and move on to the term itself. On this point, Mr. Whelan is right, at least historically. There are endless discussions about which states make up the Deep South, but by at least one definition they're the seven that left the Union prior to the firing on Fort Sumter, which are, in order of secession, South Carolina, Mississippi, Florida, Alabama, Georgia, Louisiana, and Texas.

In the century and a half since the war, the makeup of Florida has changed dramatically, but the Panhandle, bounded by Alabama to the west and the Apalachicola River to the east, remains essentially—especially—Southern. Beginning as early as 1811, its citizens lobbied to be annexed to what is now Alabama at least seven times and finally passed a successful referendum in 1869. By that time, though, Alabama's carpetbagger government rebuffed the annexation as too expensive, a blow happily remunerated almost a hundred years later by the open-ing of the Flora-Bama Lounge, which straddles the line be-tween the states.

The problem is not that the Panhandle can't be correctly called "deep southern," I just didn't know we were still being "derided" for it, and not just occasionally but "often." With the exception of some pesky periods in our not-so-distant history when we could rightly be called inhospitable or far, far worse, our good manners and friendliness have generally been consid-ered a draw. What I think Mr. Whelan really means by "deep southern feel" is "redneck reputation." Let's not forget that there's an annual mullet toss at the Flora-Bama, or that Tom T. Hall's song "Redneck Riviera" includes lyrics that recall the likes of my old friend Larry: "Nobody cares if Gramma's got a tattoo or Bubba's got a hot wing in his hand."

But Mr. Whelan has clearly not visited in a long while, if ever, because I'm worried that the redneck aspect of things is dissipating at far too fast a clip. Were she still with us, my grandmother could find plenty of dry martinis to sip on as well as swanky restaurants in which to wear her finery. Within walk-ing distance of my mother's house alone there are three places to get sushi, an amazing handmade pizza place, an organic juice bar, two wine bars, a gourmet grilled cheese stand, a James Beard–nominated restaurant, and a "shrimp shack" that sells melt-in-your-mouth lobster rolls accompanied by splits of cham-pagne. Then there are the facts that the *New York Times* regu-larly sells out by 8:00 A.M. and Sundog Books in Seaside is one of the three or four best independent bookstores in the whole country.

All of this is actually good news, especially since there's still plenty of ingrained grit and goodness to go around. Seaside's Modica Market reminds me of the family-owned Italian grocery store I grew up going to in the Delta. Charles Modica and his sister Carmel always greet me with a hug (and, usually, a draft beer on the house), but they also know to reserve some bottles of my favorite olive oil, which, until now, I've only ever found in Córdoba, Spain, and Charles's hand-cut rib eyes are the best I've ever eaten. Likewise, the weekly farmers' market features fresh eggs, collard greens, and pink-eye and purple-hull peas among the more gourmet offerings, and equidistant from the nearest sushi place is a diner that still sells deep-fried grouper on a bun. On balance this "deep southern feel," if not flat-out redneck vibe, is still working for us. Add the clearest blue-green water in the world and the powdery white sand (made of quartz washed down from the Appalachians by ancient rivers), and I'm with Tom T.: "Down here on the Redneck Riviera there ain't no better living anywhere."

The Dry County Conundrum

WHEN MY FRIEND SUZANNE RHEINSTEIN'S GORGEOUS book, *At Home*, was published, I hosted a shindig in her honor. Suzanne is a brilliant designer based in L.A., but she is from New Orleans, so to launch the book, she and her late husband, Fred, invited more than a hundred of their friends from points as far-flung as San Francisco and Paris to celebrate in her hometown. For three days, they shopped and toured and ate and drank, and by the time they got to my house on Saturday night, they'd been fully indoctrinated in the habits of the locals, from five-hour lunches at Galatoire's to "go-cups" filled with Sazeracs, everyone's new favorite drink. At the end of the first hour, the wild-eyed bartender told me we'd already gone through two cases of white wine alone; after that it was a free-for-all. By the time we finally shut down, pretty much everything in the house had been drunk, including the disgusting raspberry Stoli someone had long ago left in my freezer.

Now, I've been accused of a lot of things in my life, but having an understocked bar has never been one of them. Still, I wasn't so much embarrassed as impressed that my transplanted New Orleans friend had managed to locate such stellar running buddies. Also, there are worse things than running out of alcohol. You could, for example, live in a place where it is impossible to buy it at all.

Until recently, I hadn't thought much about what such a grim reality might be like, but, unbelievably, 18 million people who live in dry counties covering roughly 10 percent of America's landmass cope with it every day. Not surprisingly, the overwhelming majority of these folks live in the South—in Mississippi, Arkansas, Alabama, and Tennessee mostly, with Kentucky and Texas pulling up the rear—in areas where evangelical Protestants outnumber all other religions. In 2009, two political scientists from Loyola University in Chicago presented a paper with "the fundamental objective" of explaining "why certain counties persist in being 'dry' at the start of the 21st century." I can see why two guys from Illinois would be curious about this, but I could have saved them a bunch of time—"Be ye not drunk with wine," says the Bible, and there are a whole lot of people down here who still take that stuff very, very seriously.

The good professors clearly don't know any of them, because at the end of their report, they expressed profound "astonishment" over their "finding that the size of the evangelical Protestant community remains the dominant predictor of Prohibition in U.S. counties." They also made the more interesting discovery that "the presence of larger concentrations" of African Americans, and especially of Catholics, "is a powerful factor inhibiting the adoption of prohibition in a county." Since I had the good fortune to grow up in a Mississippi county which is majority black (and where Baptists were substantially outnumbered by Episcopalians and Catholics), I can happily confirm their conclusion. I had no idea that I'd been born not just in a dry county, but in a dry state, until six years after we'd legally gone wet.

Mississippi was the first state to ratify the Eighteenth Amendment, and the last to repeal Prohibition—in 1966, thirty-three years after the Twenty-first Amendment had already done so. The state legislature nonetheless found a way to tax the sale of liquor, and since nobody ever mentioned to me that it was, in fact, illegal to consume, I just assumed that liquor stores the world over delivered standing orders to your doorstep and that everybody's mothers gave the mailman a fifth of Old Crow for Christmas. Thus it came as an enormous surprise to me in 1972, when, in a state-mandated Mississippi history class, I learned that the activities of pretty much everyone I'd ever known had been against the law.

But that revelation was nothing compared to the broadside I got a few summer's back during an extended visit to Rankin County, Mississippi, whose population, it should be noted, is comprised of very few blacks and even fewer Catholics. My father had been injured in a car accident that required lengthy rehabilitation at a facility in Pearl, essentially a suburb of Jackson, the state capital, where he'd been initially hospitalized. In Jackson, the contents of a mini-fridge (some nice rosés and the white Burgundy to which my mother is partial) had not only taken the edge off the wait during the surgery that repaired his shattered hip and pelvis, but also allowed my mother and me to serve as gracious hosts to his many subsequent visitors. After he moved to Pearl, I arrived with a large ice chest I'd thoughtfully replenished on a trip home to New Orleans. I'd barely gotten back on the highway when my mother called, frantic: "It's the nurses—they're threatening to call the police about the wine."

It turned out that only beer and "light wines" (really awful coolers and other weird concoctions with absurdly low alcohol content of around 4 percent) are legal to sell or consume in Rankin County; our "real wine" was almost three times that and the staff was good at math.

When I recounted this outrage to my good friend and former *Newsweek* editor Jon Meacham, I told him, "I'd never been to Pearl until this summer," intending to finish with "And I'm sure as hell never going back." But he reminded me that I had indeed made a prior trip to Pearl. He'd sent me there himself, in 1997, to cover a shooting at Pearl High. A student had killed two classmates and wounded seven others shortly after stabbing his mother. The memory of this—and the fact that the alienated (naturally) shooter had been a member of some phony Satanist cult—made me feel strangely vindicated. "See," I said, "there you go."

Though I don't hold out much hope for Rankin County, other pockets of parched uprightness are beginning to see the light. In November 2010, for example, two counties in Arkansas voted to go wet, in part at least because of the mounting tally of fatal car crashes. In 2005, deaths related to alcohol in dry counties totaled 38 percent; by 2008, they'd climbed to

50 percent. Apparently, when people who want a drink are denied the privilege, they'll drive pretty far to get one, creating an obvious set of problems. Also, even teetotalers can understand the benefits of watering holes. The Baptist stronghold of Athens, Alabama, seat of still-dry Limestone County, voted to go wet a few years ago, and the once-dead downtown has blossomed.

It turns out that Athens is not the only place among Alabama's dry counties where you can get a drink. There are also insidious little loopholes called Community Development Districts: private residential communities with a golf course and a social club, which are allowed to serve liquor—if they have 600 members who have each paid a whopping $2,000. Surely, these insular havens of mini-Taras threaten the social fabric far more than the occasional nip of demon rum. It's no accident that in *The Second Coming*, Walker Percy, our most astute chronicler of the dangers of the New South, had Will Barrett suffer a "petty-mall" seizure on the links in precisely such a place. After briefly contemplating suicide, he "comes to himself," fleeing from his churchgoing neighbors, who were "without exception well-dressed and prosperous, healthy and happy," preferring to take up with an escaped mental patient in a greenhouse instead. It should also be noted that Percy recommended a slightly less drastic antidote to the "anomie" of "the pretty exurb" in the form of a couple of shots of Early Times. In this, I am reminded of a close family friend, the late Anne Ross McGee, whom my mother had pressed into duty to enliven a party of visiting Presbyterians. About an hour into it, I found her alone in the kitchen, determinedly knocking back Scotch.

When I asked her what she was doing, she shot me an exasperated "isn't-it-obvious-you-idiot?" kind of look. "I am trying," she said, "to drink myself some energy and personality." I am endlessly grateful that I live in a place where it is possible to do so.

The Politics of Lust

EVERY MONTH OR SO (IF I AM LUCKY), I HEAD FROM NEW Orleans to Seaside, Florida, a journey that requires me to drive (always faster than I should) across the bottom of Alabama. But on a recent trip, I was slowed down—if not altogether stopped— by the sight of a very scary billboard. Filled with screaming red letters and leaping orange flames, it did not mince words: LUST DRAGS you down to HELL. Beneath the warning, there was an 800 number to call FOR TRUTH, which presumably includes advice on how to avoid eternal torment.

It turns out that this same outfit, Christian Aid, puts up similar billboards in all fifty states, not just Alabama where I sort of expect such sightings. (According to the most recent Gallup poll, the state is tied with Mississippi as the most Protestant in the country, at 77 percent.) On its website, the group says its messages are meant to be "thought-provoking statements and questions," as well as providers of an introduction "to a God that is both loving and holy."

I have to say that the messages seem a tad more fear-inducing than loving, though I'm sure the folks on the other end of the 800 number might gently suggest that if that's so, it's because I have a lot to be afraid of. Still, another of the billboards, containing the inarguable stat that "10 out of 10 die," includes a red EKG flatline and the question "Are YOU prepared?" This is not the kind of thing that promotes highway safety. When I told my friend John Alexander about my encounter with the flames, he said he'd almost run off a Texas road a few years ago when a radio preacher repeated the question "How hot is hell? How hot is hell?" The answer: "Hell is so hot your eyeballs will melt and roll down your face."

But let's get back to lust. I'm not qualified (nor even remotely inclined) to comment on whether or not it will send you straight to hell (or toward the certain "failure and death" also promised on the ministries' website). But the facts show that it almost always sends you out of office. Take, for example, Wilbur Mills, the late former congressman from Arkansas, a state that ranks just behind Alabama and Mississippi as the most Protestant. Mills was the all-powerful, chain-smoking (Salem 100s), hard-drinking (whiskey and, it turned out, champagne) chairman of the House Ways and Means Committee when the U.S. Park Police pulled over the Lincoln Continental in which he was riding (with no headlights) around 2:00 A.M. in 1974. In the backseat, the officers (whom the congressman threatened to "demote") discovered a scratched-up Mills and his companion, Annabel Battistella, an Argentine stripper known onstage as Fanne Foxe (and forever after in the papers as "the Argentine Firecracker"). Foxe promptly jumped into the nearby tidal basin, and Mills went into hiding for a week before he appeared before the Little Rock Junior Chamber of Commerce and announced he'd learned a valuable lesson: "Don't go out with foreigners who drink champagne."

Less than a month later, he was reelected with 60 percent of the vote, and that seemed to be that until lust reared its relentless head again, along with not just a little greed and that most dangerous of all sins, chutzpah. Having accompanied Foxe to Boston, where she gave a performance at the Pilgrim Theatre, he joined her onstage mid-act and then gave a post-show interview in which he referred to her as "my little old Argentine hillbilly." He was also heard to mumble, "This won't ruin me; nothing can ruin me." It did, of course. Before the year was out, he'd been forced out of his job on Ways and Means and left the House altogether in 1976.

But greed works both ways, there are exceptions to every rule, and apparently, on earth at least, sin is negotiable. Bear with me here. In 1991, I had the distinct pleasure of covering Edwin Edwards's bid for an unprecedented fourth term as Louisiana's governor, an experience that remains some of the most fun I've ever had on or off the job. Edwards was famous for uttering a more colorful version of Mills's "nothing can ruin me" when he said that to get in trouble with the voters of his state he'd have to be found in bed "with a dead girl or a live boy." He was also a walking, talking exhibit of pretty much everything that gets the billboard people going. A big fan of cash, he checked into his favorite Las Vegas hotels (under the alias T. Wong) carrying suitcases full of the stuff, and as a young congressman he accepted a "friendship" token of $10,000 and a mink coat for his first wife from Tongsun Park of Koreagate fame.

During one of his two trials for racketeering and bribery (the first ended in a mistrial; in the second he was acquitted), he rode a donkey to the courthouse as part of a joke about the U.S. Attorney kissing his ass. On the campaign that I covered, Edwards (also known as the Silver Zipper) was accompanied by a twenty-six-year-old nursing student named Candy Picou ("At my age a man wants either a nurse or a beautiful young girlfriend. I have combined the two"). When his opponent in the runoff turned out to be the former Klansman David Duke (a sinner of a different sort), he told voters that the two had only one thing in common: "We're both wizards under the sheets." And when he won in the second biggest landslide in Louisiana history (he'd also set the record for the first), he became the first Southern governor to issue an executive order protecting lesbian, gay, bisexual, and transgender folks from discrimination in governmental services, employment, and contracts.

Far more brazenly, he dismissed the Resurrection as make-believe and, during a speech at the Gridiron Club of Alexandria, one of the most conservative and heavily Protestant pockets of the state, mocked the Crucifixion with a lipstick and ketchup stigmata. When I later accompanied him to an appearance at one of the city's largest Pentecostal churches, I was astonished to find an enormous crowd and a whole roster of effusive preachers. When I asked one of them how he squared support of Edwards with his views, the man provided me with what became a stock answer among the clergy: "Well, he doesn't drink or smoke." More to the point, as governor, Edwards had provided this particular church with a waiver enabling the congregation to get around a law requiring the installation of an expensive sprinkler system.

In the end, Edwards was right—it wasn't the voters who got him, it was the feds, who take a slightly less nuanced view of sin. They also really, really dislike losing. After decades of trying and failing to convict Edwards of something—anything—they spent a whole bunch of money and gave a whole bunch of bad guys immunity in order to nail him on the charge of accepting bribes in exchange for riverboat casino licenses. Even though he wasn't even governor anymore, he was sentenced to a decade in prison. The lesson here is that a U.S. Attorney with a vendetta and endless pockets of our tax dollars at work is far more terrifying than the devil himself. But even prison did not manage to dim the former governor's lustful ways. Not long after his release in 2011, he married—at eighty-three—his third wife, Trina, a former prison pen pal fifty-two years his junior.

In 2013, the couple had a son, Eli, and a year later Edwards ran for his old seat in Congress. Although he didn't win, he made the runoff and attracted lots of the old adoring crowds. The women said they admired his honesty—if he gambled, he was up-front about it, after all, and if he stole, he stole from fat cats and not the taxpayers. The men, both covetous and lusty, mostly ogled the very hot Trina. Which brings us back to the subject of the flaming billboard and a story from my time covering fashion rather than politics.

It was 1992, a year after Edwards's fourth win and a week after Bill Clinton's first as president, and I'd been dispatched to Paris, where I attended a Chanel fashion show that featured a parade of models wearing nothing below the waist but skirts made of clear inner tubes, the kind little kids swim in. Such was (and is) the power of Chanel's designer Karl Lagerfeld, the show ushered in a couple of seasons of transparent clothing. But that wasn't what I remember most about the event, at which my companions included my then *Vogue* colleague André Leon Talley and his friend, a Hollywood producer who, like me, had been raised in the Mississippi Delta. As usual, after the show the fashion press and assorted hangers-on pushed backstage for pronouncements from the master: "Karl, Karl, what does it all mean?" Sunglasses firmly in place, Lagerfeld uttered a single sentence: "Poossy is in." While everyone else dutifully digested this information, our Mississippi pal felt the need to put things in perspective. A sophisticated fellow, he wore custom Versace suits and had a lovely car and driver, but he grew up in a place where people didn't say that kind of stuff and definitely not about fashion. "Damn," he roared. "I never knew it went out." Indeed. Lust, it seems, is a trend for the ages—one that no amount of hair-raising highway art will likely curb.

Good Country, Bad Behavior

IN 2012 AND 2013, ALMOST FOUR MONTHS TO THE DAY apart, two people who had a profound influence on my life died: Jean Harris, eighty-nine, my headmistress at Virginia's Madeira School who was referred to derisively as Integrity Jean; and George Jones, eighty-one, who was, well, George Jones and referred to good-naturedly as No-Show Jones and the Possum. Jones's song "He Stopped Loving Her Today" is arguably the best country music recording ever made, and the sausage sold under his name was so good I wrote a *New York Times* column about it. (The inclusion of a recipe for sausage balls, a Deep South cocktail party stalwart Jones had never heard of, prompted the following outbursts from the man himself: "I've got the sausage and I've got the balls—*ha!*" and, "Say, Mama, they're burning up my sausage. . . . Don't worry about your sausage, son, you better worry about your balls.") But despite the countless hours of entertainment (both musical and comical) I've derived from Jones, Harris's influence was rather more dramatic: Had she not murdered Herman Tarnower, her longtime lover and author of the wildly successful *The Complete Scarsdale Medical Diet*, I might not have had a career.

This, in a—sort of—nutshell, is what happened: During my junior year at Madeira, the almost entirely all-male board decided with typical wisdom to replace our brilliant but decidedly masculine headmistress (who went on to become town supervisor of Shelter Island, New York) with Jean Harris, even though her most recent job had been manager of sales at a Manhattan-based company that sold cleaning contracts to office buildings, and when I later interviewed a former board member at a previous school where she'd been head, he blamed her for its ultimate demise. When she was introduced on the hockey field during the spring Fathers' Weekend (in a bow to the number of divorced parents, the traditional Parents' Weekend had been split in two), I took one look at her, turned to my father, and said, "One day they are going to come get that woman in a truck."

My father, like most of the rest of the assembled dads, had already pronounced her "attractive" in her knockoff Chanel suit, and mumbled something about my dislike of authority (which is not exactly true—I just prefer it when the people nominally in charge of my well-being possess some modicum of sanity). At any rate, the following year proved my instincts right. She walked through campus head down, yanking at her hair; once, at a "relaxed" meeting at her house, she sat with us on the floor and pulled up huge clumps of carpet. We had no way of knowing that she was taking the methamphetamine Desoxyn (along with Valium, Percodan, Nembutal, and other goodies revealed to have been in her medicine cabinet), or that she was in the grips of an increasingly desperate obsession with the famous Dr. Tarnower.

Whereas her predecessor didn't much care what we did as long as we worked our asses off academically, Harris clearly had more literal goals in that department. She put the entire school on what turned out to be the Scarsdale Diet, she hammered incessantly at our general lack of ladylikeness, and twice in her yearbook letter to our graduating class, she underlined the importance of a "stout heart." No wonder—in a scenario familiar to country music fans everywhere, it turns out that she was being eclipsed in Tarnower's affections by his younger, blonder office assistant, a woman whom the high-minded Harris derided in a letter to her lover as "tasteless," "ignorant," "cutesie," and, for good measure, "a slut." It was the latter's frilly negligee and pink curlers that Harris spotted in Tarnower's bathroom on that night in 1980 when she pumped three bullets into his chest from several feet away, an occurrence she forever termed a "tragic accident."

By then I was a sophomore at Georgetown and a part-time library assistant/phone answerer at *Newsweek*'s Washington bureau, a job I'd gotten via Madeira's ingenious cocurriculum program, in which the students are bused off to D.C.-area internships once a week. On the morning after Harris shot Tarnower, the bureau chief woke me up with an order to get out to my old school. When I asked him why on earth, he barked, "You idiot, your headmistress just shot the diet doctor."

Looking back, I realize I had none of the usual reactions. Instead, I threw on clothes, jumped in the car, made my way past the guards (with whom I'd made sure to be on extraordinarily good terms during my slightly shady school tenure), and got the scoop on all that had transpired before Harris drove off campus armed with a gun. On the way back, I stopped at a pay phone to make an especially fulfilling "I told you so" call to my father (even the truck part was right—deliciously, Harris had been transported from the crime scene in an old-fashioned paddy wagon). Then I typed up my notes, filed my story to New York, and got my first-ever byline. I was nineteen and only the tiniest bit sorry that the good doctor had given his life in service to my future as a journalist.

It has been during that career that I've had the privilege of meeting many a country music great, including Jones, largely through my friend Susan Nadler, to whom Jones referred to with affection as "my little Jew" and who was also part owner of his record company. Susan has worked with everyone from Willie Nelson and Kris Kristofferson to Tammy Wynette (Jones's third wife and singing partner) and is herself no stranger to crime. She once did time in a Mexican jail, an experience immortalized in a memoir called *The Butterfly Convention*, and she wrote another fine book, *Good Girls Gone Bad*, in which Harris could easily have been a chapter. Anyway, just before Jones died, he sent Susan a letter promising her a spot next to Johnny Paycheck in his private group of cemetery plots, and while we were cracking up over that, um, generous offer, among other evidence of Jones's decidedly off-kilter but weirdly sweet nature, it occurred to me that Jean and George had more in common than might initially be apparent.

Harris was born in an affluent suburb of Cleveland, Ohio, while Jones was born in an area outside of Beaumont, Texas, known as the Big Thicket. Harris went to Smith College and graduated magna cum laude; Jones went to Jasper, Texas, where he played and sang on KTXJ radio. Which is why it is always instructive to go deeper. For one thing, the emotional use of a firearm landed them both in a lot of trouble. Jones shot up an untold amount of hotel rooms, some houses, the floor of one of his tour buses, and the car of his good buddy Peanut Montgomery, for which he got slapped with an attempted murder charge that was later dropped. And while the only room we know for sure Harris shot up was her boyfriend's Scarsdale bedroom, it turned out to be enough, since it landed her in a women's prison for twelve years.

Then, of course, there was the fondness for drugs (Jones preferred cocaine and whiskey over Harris's pills) and the resulting paranoia. Jones was variously convinced that monsters were crawling in his car or that he'd been targeted by the mob, and he was once carted off in a straitjacket. For her part, Harris accused her rival of subjecting her to all sorts of indignities, including cutting up her clothes—though Harris herself had cut up a needlepoint rug made by yet another woman whom the doc had earlier dated, and mailed the pieces back to her in a shoebox. When it came to tortuous love affairs, Jones, not surprisingly, took a more direct approach—on the night he took Tammy away from her then husband, he simply turned over a dining room table and shot the lamp.

It was always said of Jones that he was such an astonishingly moving interpreter of country songs because he'd lived most of their content, but plenty of Jones's titles (if not the exact lyrics) could have been applied to Harris's tawdry saga. "She Thinks I Still Care," "Why Baby Why," and, of course, "He Stopped Loving Her Today" come immediately to mind.

Harris wrote that she found redemption (even though she never actually admitted guilt—she was, she said instead, an "instrument" in Tarnower's death) by campaigning for a nursery for the children of fellow inmates. That's nice, but I'll take Jones's 100-plus albums and unmistakable voice filled with that aching vulnerability and full-on heart—qualities the jury could never locate in Harris, who wore fur-collared coats and an air of superiority to court every day.

With heart also comes humor, and the all-important ability to laugh at oneself. During our first interview, I had to confess to Jones that I'd run over one of the newly installed lights in his driveway. "That's okay," he shot back, "I'm partial to guardrails myself." It was a hilarious afternoon (before he even agreed to return home from his daily lunch at Subway, he had to be reassured I wasn't a Yankee), punctuated by the Jones magic. At one point he broke into a spine-tingling a cappella version of Don Gibson's "I Can't Stop Loving You." It's not a bad epitaph for both Harris and Jones—for the former, one leaning toward the bitterly ironic, and for the latter, entirely fitting. Those close to Jones say he never completely let go of the torch he carried for Wynette, and he certainly held on to his deep love for "true" country and his sainted fourth wife, Nancy, who is credited with keeping him—mostly—straight, and who will be buried beside him.

Hollywood on the Delta

IN 2014 AT THE SECOND ANNUAL DELTA HOT TAMALE Festival in Greenville, Mississippi, there was a kickoff party for the visiting writers and chefs at what we locals refer to as the Baby Doll House. The party, designed and catered by my friends Amanda and Carl Cottingham, was stunning, as was the setting. Guests arrived just as the sinking sun had turned the sky a gorgeous fuchsia and an enormous harvest moon was on the rise. The house, a majestic three-story Greek Revival, appeared like an apparition in the middle of hundreds of acres of cotton and soybeans. Eden Brent dazzled with her trademark rollicking blues piano from the front porch, and two bars flanked the entrance.

It was a really, really good party, but for a lot of the guests who made the trek to Benoit, the tiny Mississippi Delta town along the river where the house is located, the history of the place was as alluring as the shindig. Completed in 1861 by

Judge J. C. Burrus, the home was spared destruction by the Yankees thanks to the fact that the commander of the Union troops in the area had befriended the judge while at the University of Virginia. During the war, it became a makeshift hospital for hundreds of Confederate troops; after Lee's surrender, General Jubal Early hid out there before being secretly transported across the Mississippi by his host.

Most tantalizing, though, was the fact that it served as the location for the 1956 film *Baby Doll*, a mashup of two Tennessee Williams one-act plays, *27 Wagons Full of Cotton* and *The Long Stay Cut Short*, that starred Karl Malden, Carroll Baker, and Eli Wallach in his very first film role. The movie was billed as "Elia Kazan's production of Tennessee Williams' boldest story," with the "boldest" part driven home by its poster, featuring the twenty-five-year-old Baker (in the title role) wearing what is now universally known as a "baby doll" nightgown, curled up in a crib, and rather provocatively sucking her thumb.

Since Benoit is only twenty miles from my hometown of Greenville, I'd heard the stories all my life. The cast and crew had camped out for months on end at the Greenville Hotel downtown and dined out almost nightly at Doe's Eat Place. Malden, who played Archie Lee Meighan, Baby Doll's frustrated husband, went deer hunting with my best friend's grandfather Jesse Brent, while Eades Hogue, the uncle of another close friend, was cast in the role of town marshal. My father, a habitué of a "tonk" called Mink's, frequently spotted Williams among the crowd there, and on a particularly frigid day, he and a friend slipped onto the set to watch Malden jump out of the house with a gun in pursuit of his nemesis, Wallach. "It was cold as hell and he had to do it five or six times in a row.

I said, 'Man, this movie stuff is tough.'" (Though the story was set in summer, the movie was filmed during a cold snap so brutal that the actors had to suck on ice cubes to keep their breath from showing.)

Kazan and his wife stayed at the house of Hodding Carter II, the editor of the local *Delta Democrat-Times* who'd won a Pulitzer ten years earlier for editorials championing racial tolerance. After a raucous Thanksgiving feast at the Carters' home, their teenage son Philip was enlisted to drive Baker back to the hotel. "She was trying to draw me out and asked me what kind of car I'd like to have one day," he remembers. "I was so tongue-tied, I finally spluttered 'a Buick.' It was the most uncool reaction I could've had."

Philip's nephew Hodding Carter IV was one of the featured authors at the tamale party, and we both realized that while we'd heard all the lore surrounding the movie, we'd never actually watched it. So I did. And man, no wonder people persist in thinking of us Delta folk as decadent. When the film came out, *Time* described it as "just possibly the dirtiest American-made motion picture that has ever been legally exhibited." Francis Cardinal Spellman pronounced it "evil in concept" and "certain to exert an immoral and corrupting influence upon those who see it."

For those who have not been so corrupted, allow me to recap: The witless, down-on-his-luck Archie Lee marries the seventeen-year-old Baby Doll but promises her dying father he won't consummate the marriage—or indeed, lay a hand on her—until her twentieth birthday. As the big day approaches, a rival owner of a more modern cotton gin, the Sicilian Silva Vacarro (Wallach), has usurped all of Archie's business, the

Ideal Pay As You Go Plan Furniture Company arrives to re-possess all five sets of furniture in the house, and Baby Doll threatens to leave (one of the stipulations of the marriage agreement is that the house be fully furnished). Archie Lee retaliates by burning down Vacarro's gin, and Vacarro proceeds to try to seduce Baby Doll—not for sex necessarily, but so that she'll sign an affidavit confirming Archie Lee's guilt.

You sort of have to see it to figure out what got the good cardinal so bent out of shape. The movie opens with a hot and bothered Malden watching Baker through a hole in the wall of the adjoining room. Wallach, who says *Baby Doll* is his favorite of all his films, spends more time in the crib than Baker. Baby Doll drinks Cokes for breakfast and all but makes love to an ice cream cone as poor Archie Lee laments, "There's no torture on earth to equal the torture which a cold woman inflicts on a man."

Despite its outrageous components, the movie is actually not campy at all, but pretty great, and all manner of really smart people are obsessed with it. Not long ago, I interviewed John Mellencamp, rocker, painter, occasional actor, and, as it happens, avid old-movie buff, about something else entirely, but before the conversation was over, we'd somehow gotten onto the film. Impressively, Mellencamp can quote whole chunks of dialogue, including one in which Vacarro comforts Baby Doll about the fact that she never made it past fourth grade: "I don't think you need to worry about your failure at long division. I mean, after all, you got through short division, and short division is all that a lady ought to be called on to cope with."

Clearly, *Time* and Cardinal Spellman did not have much of a sense of humor, but neither did countless others, including the Legion of Decency, which denounced the film with a C rating (for condemned). One of the critics who managed to suss out its more "sardonic" qualities was the *New York Times's* Bosley Crowther, who declared that given the nature of the folks involved they'd be "unendurable" shaped by a less talented pen. "Williams has written his trashy, vicious people so that they are clinically interesting. And Karl Malden, Carroll Baker, Mildred Dunnock and Eli Wallach have acted them, under Mr. Kazan's superb direction, so that they nigh corrode the screen." But it's the house that comes off best: "Mr. Kazan's pictorial compositions, got in stark black-and-white and framed for the most part against the background of an old Mississippi mansion, are by far the most artful, and respectable, feature of *Baby Doll.*"

My father, whose memory is usually infallible, insists that Kazan returned to Greenville a year later with his daughter to have her presented at the Delta Debutante Ball. None of the ladies on the Society's current board can find evidence confirming that rather unlikely turn of events, but in a weird way, it would have been fitting. After all, the debs, done up in all those big white dresses covered with loads of embroidery and lace, look a lot like dolls, and are meant to be as virginal as Baker. Also, for years, my parents and our friends the McGees referred to the annual presentation as the Baby Tot Ball, a moniker inspired by the McGees' babysitter Mary Bell, who kept Anne and Elizabeth McGee and me when the grown-ups attended the annual event and who misheard the real name as they went out the door. Everyone decided Mary Bell's version was far more fitting, and my father subsequently immortalized it as a verb, as in we're going "babytotting."

It turns out that Williams, who spent a lot of time in New Orleans, could have been inspired by a whole group of grown women there who dressed as baby dolls. In 1912, like the rest of the city, the red-light district was divided along racial lines and there was a rivalry between the two groups of prostitutes. When the black women heard that their white counterparts were going to mask and parade during Mardi Gras, they decided to outdo them, according to Kim Vaz, a dean at Louisiana's Xavier University who has written a book on the subject. "They said, 'Let's just be baby dolls because that's what the men call us,'" Vaz recounts, adding that their outfits consisted of short satin skirts with bloomers.

I'm happy to report that things in the world of baby dolls have come full circle. A few years ago, a New Orleans choreographer resurrected the Baby Doll maskers, and now they march in the Zulu parade. And the Baby Doll House, which sat fallow for decades and lost its facade in a 2001 tornado, was beautifully restored two years ago by the heirs of Judge Burrus, including my friend Eustace Winn, who rents it out for parties like the one during the tamale fest. Perhaps someone will throw an appropriate fete during the coming season for one of the Delta's lovely debs, aka Baby Tots. It's just too bad that Baker's crib is long gone from the premises.

When the Sun
Don't Shine

YEARS AGO, A FRIEND GAVE ME A BASEBALL CAP EMBLA-
zoned with the phrase "American by Birth, Southern by the
Grace of God." I love that cap. I'm pretty sure I've mentioned
it in this space before because it sums up how I feel about my
native region. Most of the time. There are, alas, some queasy
moments, those dread occasions when the shenanigans of some
of our inhabitants make me feel as though I might have been
born under a bad sign—or flag, as it were. The third week of
Jimmy Fallon's triumphant debut as host of *The Tonight Show*
was just such a time.

It had been a pretty good week so far. New Orleans was in
the midst of Mardi Gras celebrations and I'd had the honor of
being selected Honorary Muse in the very cool Muses parade,
for which I'd made a lovely headdress out of a leopard print bra
from Walmart, a purple-satin-and-crystal Manolo Blahnik
shoe buckle, and a handful of ostrich feathers. I got to ride in a

gigantic red shoe while two very nice crimson-wigged minions handed me beads and bracelets and cups and glittered shoes to throw to the thousands of pumped-up parade goers lining St. Charles Avenue. As anyone who has done it will tell you, it's the closest the rest of us will ever get to being Bruce Springsteen. So I was still in a giddy mood the following evening after some parade watching of my own.

That's when it happened. I was enjoying a civilized nightcap with my good friend Elizabeth McGee Cordes when her sister Anne came hollering down the stairs from the guest room where she was bunking. She dragged us back up to the TV on which she had recorded the last bits of Fallon's monologue, which turned out to be a Trifecta of the Embarrassing South: Honey Boo Boo's Mama June discussing her sex life with her older daughter, the confused Pumpkin ("Wham bam what?"); the Mississippi coroner who pronounced a live man dead and sent him—in a zipped-up body bag—to the funeral home; and Paula Deen, who declared her comeback at a Miami food festival by mounting and riding Food Network chef Robert Irvine, who was on all fours on the stage.

Our initial collective reaction was not unlike that of Fallon, who knew he'd hit such gold that he just stood there speechless and wide-eyed for a full beat. After the astonishing clip of Paula's ride, he did manage to quip that "even Mama June was like, 'Ew.'" But let's take it from the top. I had heard of Honey Boo Boo, of course, but had carefully avoided actually watching the show, which I was shocked to discover is broadcast on TLC. For obvious reasons the network no longer refers to itself as The Learning Channel, but you could make the case that the exploits of this particular bunch demonstrate to the rest of the country what is meant by Peckerwood Mayhem, a terrifyingly apt term coined by my buddy the *Thacker Mountain Radio* host Jim Dees. Mere words really cannot do justice to the clip Fallon showed, but then words apparently are a problem on the show generally. As Fallon pointed out, *Here Comes Honey Boo Boo* uses subtitles even though it is broadcast in English (sort of).

Then came the second bit, which hit a tad too close to home for the McGee girls and me, since it occurred in our home state, Mississippi, in a town, Lexington, that is not all that far from our own. Since Fallon didn't get into the details of the premature death pronouncement, we immediately Googled the story and came across a trove of information, the kind you really can't make up. Fallon really sort of wasted an opportunity by not devoting his entire monologue to the story of how Walter Williams, a farmer and family man who was admittedly very sick, ended up at Porter and Sons on the embalming table.

First, there's the fact that Holmes County turns out to have the lowest life expectancy rate, among both men and women, of any county in the entire United States—a fact, we conjectured, that might be explained by the coroner's apparent knack for declaring live people dead. Second, this same coroner shares a first name, Dexter, with cable television's most beloved serial killer—a pleasing irony, really, unless you happened to be Mr. Williams. This particular Dexter (last name Howard), like all coroners in Mississippi, is an elected official. He also does not happen to be in possession of a medical degree. When he felt for a pulse and couldn't find one, he shipped poor Mr. Williams, who later said he'd been taking a nap, off to the mortuary, where the owner, Byron Porter, said he was a couple of minutes away ("no more than that") from the embalming needle. Then his legs began to move. "We noticed his legs . . . like kicking," the coroner told local news channel WAPT. "He also began to do a little breathing." Mr. Porter was a bit more succinct: "He was not dead, long story short," he said, noting that at that point it was unanimously decided that they would not inject him with embalming fluid.

Under the circumstances, the family of Mr. Williams, who has since passed away for sure, has been remarkably gracious, expressing gratitude for the extra time with their loved one as well as for the outpouring of public support after the news broke. When asked what happened, the coroner opined that Williams's pacemaker might have stopped working for a bit or that it was just a flat-out miracle. "I've never seen anything like it." Either way, as Anne herself opined, the whole episode gives new urgency to the saying "shake a leg."

Finally, we come to Paula, the gift that keeps on giving. She'd already been on my mind that week because one of the more hilarious and spot-on Muses floats had been devoted to the brouhaha that got her booted off the Food Network in the summer of 2013. The parade this year was all about fashion ("Off the Rack and Ready to Wear You Out"), and the Paula float was the fittingly titled "Separates." Riders wore white wigs with headpieces made of red lips swallowing a stick of butter (a suggestive image not unlike the Rolling Stones' Hot Licks logo first used on the album cover for *Sticky Fingers*), while the sides of the float itself were decorated with images of white meat, white beans, blond brownies, Aryan 100% White Sugar, and a quote reading, "Y'all, in the South, we don't mix and match."

The Muses parade is one of the few that still carry on the long and welcome tradition of Mardi Gras satire, and plenty of folks, including then Louisiana governor Bobby Jindal, who rated an "Insincere Sucker" float, got equal treatment. I know Paula still has legions of fans, and I'm sure those who saw the float objected to it, but I mean . . . seriously. I will confess up front to my own classism when it comes to Paula, because those weird blue contacts and that cloying accent and all those diamond rings on her fingers while she's kneading dough got on my nerves long before she—well, pick a transgression. But it must be said that she is not her own best advocate. At the South Beach Wine & Food Festival, she did a demo on the *Today* show during which she made so many raunchy jokes about "chicken balls," the name of the dish she was cooking, that Al Roker finally said, "Set your watches; that's where it all went wrong." Nah, I'm pretty sure that had happened the day before when she hopped onto Irvine's back and shouted, "Giddy up, I'm back in the saddle."

At first the clips from Fallon's monologue put me in mind of the scene in *The Last Picture Show* in which the late great Ben Johnson tells Timothy Bottoms, "I've been around that trashy behavior all my life. I'm gettin' tired of puttin' up with it." But then I was reminded that pretty much everybody puts up with it at one point or another. A few nights after the fateful Fallon show, Jimmy Kimmel hosted Toronto's crack-smoking, hard-drinking, seemingly insane mayor Rob Ford, who also had a bad moment in Florida, where he was charged with marijuana possession and DUI. Ford's over-the-top antics, which involve racist, homophobic, and misogynistic outbursts far too lengthy to go into here, are enough to give even Mama June pause. Apparently, Peckerwood Mayhem knows no boundaries.

Part Five

Fun

Hell on Wheels

MY 1978 TOYOTA CELICA WAS NOT MY FIRST CAR, BUT IT was *the* car, the one that defined (indeed, made possible) my late teens and early twenties. Black and sporty with a sunroof and a speedometer that hit 120 in no time flat, it was a gift from my parents when I graduated from boarding school. My very nice mother drove it up from Greenville, Mississippi, to McLean, Virginia, just so my friend Courtney and I could drive it back—the first of countless badly planned and/or thoroughly ill-advised road trips that car would make (to New Orleans to see the Rolling Stones, to Maine to see a dangerous man with whom I was briefly but madly in love, to Detroit for the convention that nominated Reagan). Eight years later, I sold it in Orlando, Florida, where I worked at the newspaper. The man at the Toyota lot I brought it to first barely took a look before steering me to a scrap dealer who gave me sixty-five dollars, way more than I actually thought I'd get. My sweet Celica had been far kinder to me than I ever was to it.

Though I was seventeen when I got it, there had already been plenty of significant automobiles in my life. There was my Nashville grandfather's Thunderbird, complete with an engraved plaque ("Made especially for G. Daniel Brooks . . .") I thought was the height of cool, and my grandmother's charcoal Cadillac Fleetwood, the enormous trunk of which was always filled with country hams and caramel cakes and dozens of gold-wrapped presents when it pulled into our driveway every other Christmas. One of my very first crushes drove a rust Gran Torino with a yellow flame down the side (I later shifted my allegiance to the owner of a rather more tasteful Torino in baby blue), while my first great love owned a very handy yellow Volkswagen Bus.

My parents' autos were decidedly less memorable, due mainly to my father's notorious cheapness and an ego whose robust health has never been tied to cars. My mother received one of the nicer station wagons of my childhood, a glittery blue Impala, when its previous owner, who had worked for my father, dropped dead of a heart attack. Such was its relative newness that Mama was inspired to take my cousin and me on a road trip out West, but the car's looks were deceiving. We spent whole days touring the garages of Tyler, Texas, and Flagstaff, Arizona.

When I turned fifteen (then the driving age in Mississippi), my father bought me a navy 1967 Mustang for four hundred dollars. In my first year of ownership I'm sure I put at least fifty thousand miles on that car without ever leaving the Mississippi Delta. It had a convertible top, the requisite eight-track tape player, and a metal ashtray so deep it could (and did) hold a carton of Marlboro Red cigarette butts at a time. During my senior year of high school, Daddy sold it (with my favorite silver earrings and a bottle of contraband whiskey still in the glove compartment), and I was so mad I ceased to speak to him for a month. But then he made up for it with the brand-new Celica, such a phenomenally unlikely choice that it still baffles me.

What I did not get was any instruction on the care and feeding of an automobile. I didn't have any idea, for example, that you were supposed to change the oil—or what that even meant. I found out seven years and well over a hundred thousand miles later when the Celica died at the drive-through window of a Winter Park, Florida, Steak 'n Shake. The man at the Shell station across the street took a long look at the engine and an even longer look at me. "Ma'am," he said, "if this car were a child, you'd be in jail." But then he got it running again and off I went. By that time, the floorboards were no longer level because whole layers of lichen—I swear—had grown underneath the carpet. Apparently, within my first few months of ownership, Toyota had sent out a notice informing buyers of a tiny malfunction involving the rubber seal of the trunk that I'd either missed or ignored. This meant that every time it rained, the water would run off into a sort of narrow trough that directed it to the floors of the passenger sides of the front and back seats, where it sat for so long things finally began to grow. It took six or seven years, but one day I noticed something slimy protruding from the carpet, and when I tried to pick it up I realized it was attached to a hard bed lurking beneath.

But really, the lichen was the least of it. Right off the bat, it was as though that car gave me carte blanche to behave as irresponsibly as humanly possible. The first month I had it, I left a rather raucous swimming party on the opposite side of town from home (where I was already an hour or so past curfew) and decided that my hair would dry faster through the sunroof, especially if I was going really, really fast and ignored a couple of stop signs and a light. The cop who pulled me over was unamused by my outfit (damp bathing suit) or my hair (dried straight up in a Bride of Frankenstein do) and carted me off to the jail. I dared not call my father, but he somehow got word of my incarceration and was so suffused with disgust when he arrived at the police station that the memory of his face still scares the bejesus out of me almost forty years later.

That fall I loaded the Celica with a metal footlocker, my stereo, and a box of LPs and drove myself to college at Georgetown, where I became instantly popular with my fellow students who had abided by the rule prohibiting freshmen from having cars. The road trips commenced in earnest. There was the night (after an extremely festive time of it at the Tombs or the Third Edition, I can't remember which) Bryan Carey, son of then governor of New York Hugh Carey, and I decided it would be a great idea to hit the road right then and there for Albany to surprise his dad. When we left, our compatriots had to push us down the hill on O Street just to jump the car, the first sign that our outing might not be the best idea. Then there was the Sunday that a housemate's buddy had gotten picked up by the state police for hitchhiking in Kentucky. Clearly, we had to rescue him, and besides, one of our group had a sheet of blotter acid, so we could combine two trips in one. I have a vague recollection that the acid trip, which I'd never tried before, was like the road trip—I mostly wished them both to be over. Far more memorable was the discovery of the just-invented Hardee's breakfast biscuit, which might well have saved us and which remains one of the great rewards of long nights on the road.

Most of the trips involved the thousand-mile-plus trek home to the Delta from D.C., most often accompanied by my thirty-five-pound long-haired cat, Sam, acquired during my sophomore year, and my most stalwart (to this day) traveling companion, Anne Flaherty, who seemed to every parent (including my own) to be the responsible one, while in reality she was every bit as bad as I was, especially in the car maintenance department. Once, when she took the Celica to our neighborhood service station (when such a thing existed), the Iranian pumping the gas asked her if she'd like him to check the brake fluid. When Anne, busy sunning herself through the open roof, replied with a blasé "I guess," he became enraged. "You *guess*? You *guess*? You do not *guess* with your *life!*" The guy was perhaps a tad edgy since it had only been a couple of years since the Ayatollah Khomeini had driven the shah—and him—from his home country, but he had a point. I only wish he'd told me about that oil change thing.

Anyway, we did a lot of guessing with our lives, most notably when we left for Christmas break during an especially cold December. Having spent the evening at Nathan's, where Anne was employed as the record girl (she sat in a booth and spun records for the customers in the dining room while I dutifully waited for her in the bar), we got a bit of a late start, which meant that it was about 10:00 P.M. when we departed. We were seriously short on cash (I think we had seven dollars between us), but we figured we'd be okay with Anne's father's Amoco credit card and the three tangerines and bottle of sherry we'd scrounged for sustenance. Then, somewhere in the mountains of Virginia, we had a blowout.

Now, I had taken driver's ed from our school's assistant football coach the summer before I got my license, but I had no idea how to change a tire, and our situation suddenly had me feeling slighted. The thinking at the time had been that if you flirted with Coach O'Brien, he wouldn't make you learn how, but in retrospect I realize it was because he was carrying two or three spare tires of his own around his middle and he had no more desire to get out into the punishing June heat and humidity than we did. Anne was similarly lacking in this rather crucial skill set, and there was also the problem of locating the jack and the spare in the first place. Since we'd been too under the weather to actually pack, all our clothes and shoes and undergarments had been thrown, loose, into the trunk, and we had to mound them up on the side of the very empty road. After at least an inch of snow had fallen on our belongings and us, and more than a dozen truckers had wisely chosen not to get mixed up with our madness, a lone savior stopped and changed our tire while we held his lighter (which we subsequently lost) so he could see. Soon after we crossed into Tennessee, an Amoco station shone like a beacon, and when we came out, with bulging armloads of Doritos and cigarettes and beer and Snickers, it looked as though we'd robbed the place.

Our Southern odysseys went on for years on end—even after I moved to Orlando, we took the Celica all the way down to Key West—and almost always involved at least one speeding ticket (each) per trip. We racked up so many in the tiny Delta town of Beulah (in our defense, it's extremely hard to realize it's a town) we ended up cutting a deal with the justice of the peace, trading pecan pies from Greenville's Sherman's grocery store for the tearing up of the tickets.

I thought about the late Judge Arnold the other day (actually, I think about him a lot since the lawyer who facilitated the transaction, my old friend George F. "Boo" Hollowell, Jr., once gave me a julep cup inscribed with the words *Judge W. D. Arnold Memorial Speedway* that currently holds the pens on my desk). Anyway, I was blowing through his old hometown doing my usual ninety when some part of my reptilian brain kicked in and urged me to slow down. There were no cops in sight, but I had to smile at how little my so-called adult life has evolved. For one thing, I was driving a black car with the sunroof wide open, and Bonnie Raitt, Anne's and my preferred traveling music, was blaring from the stereo. The car is now a Caddy rather than a Celica (but it's the first new car I've owned since), and Bonnie's excellent *Dig In Deep* was playing on SiriusXM rather than a cassette player. It's no wonder that I take solace in the facts that Boo still maintains a practice in Greenville and Sherman's, though now a restaurant, makes the same pecan pie.

Though I still spend a ton of time on Mississippi's byways, it has been a while since Anne and I have hit the road together. Our most recent trips have required commercial air travel, including one to Madrid a few years ago when the sherry I was sipping reminded me of our escapades. We took a lighthearted look down some of our more harrowing lanes and then I actually said something like, "Yeah, but there was always one thing about us. We were smart enough not to go completely over the edge. We instinctively knew when to pull back, when not to go too far." At this patently ridiculous statement, Anne's right eyebrow shot up past her hairline and she gave me a look only someone who has known you so long and so deep can give. Then we laughed so hard the entire tapas bar turned to stare. We both knew that we'd been idiots, that the grace of God and dumb luck were the only reasons I'd lived long enough to say something so pompous and she'd lived long enough to hear it. That is: the grace of God, dumb luck, and the power of the mighty Celica, so mistreated yet so giving.

One for the Road

THERE'S A SCENE IN WALKER PERCY'S *LOVE IN THE RUINS* in which the protagonist, Dr. Tom More, is holed up in the Paradise Estates pro shop with a skinny black kid named Elzee Acree and the slightly unhinged white Colonel Ringo, who has been defending the Christian Kaydettes from Bantu snipers (the book, it should be noted, is set during "a Time Near the End of the World"). In addition to the fact that Percy has here written some of the funniest passages in all of American literature, he highlights two of the more time-honored means by which the average Southerner has managed to enjoy a much-needed drink of whiskey. First, when Tom arrives at the pro shop, he has on his person a pint-size flask—in fact, he has it always, as did, presumably, the young Walker Percy, who grew up in Mississippi at a time when the Early Times both he and Tom preferred was not legally available. Then there is the restorative concoction requested by the colonel after a bullet grazes his private parts: "Bring me a 7 Up, Elzee. . . . Now pour out the neck and fill it up from Doc's bottle there."

"Pour out the neck." The very phrase is proof of Percy's unerring ear and flashes back to teenage dances and Friday nights hanging out with the bad boys underneath the football bleachers before anybody knew how to buy marijuana. A spiked 7 Up, Coca-Cola, or Dr Pepper remains the perfect beverage for foxhole moments, hot days, rural road trips, and places where it is still not very acceptable to be seen imbibing.

Of course, in New Orleans, where I live and near where Percy set his novel, there are few places where the latter is the case. It is legal to drink on the streets, and people persist in drinking while they're driving. They bring their own drinks into restaurants, and they take the restaurants' drinks out. The most popular—indeed, beloved—receptacle for all this activity is the plastic or Styrofoam "go cup" (or, to use one of the hokier monikers lately emblazoned on the thing itself, a "Geaux Cup").

They are in use 24/7, but the time to stock up is Mardi Gras. Since each krewe prints up its own versions and uses them as "throws," a particularly energetic and focused parade-goer can catch up to a year's supply. More useful than beads and doubloons or the occasional rubber chicken, they can also be put to immediate good use. In fact, pretty much the only people during a Mardi Gras parade not holding a cup are the riders themselves, who wear the adult versions of sippy cups around their necks so that their hands remain free for throwing. (My ex-husband once rigged up a pedal-operated contraption that sent a fairly steady stream of alcohol into his mouth via a rubber tube that snaked up through his costume—a stroke of ingenuity that may explain why, toward the end of his ride, he hung upside down from his harness without realizing that he was doing so.)

But New Orleans is certainly not the only place where people tote their drinks around. Every single afternoon of my childhood, my father came home from his office, mixed a couple of martinis in the glazed McCarty's pottery wine cups he and my mother received as wedding presents, and took them with him to pick up his best friend, Nick. The glazed clay kept the drinks cool while they sipped and talked and drove down Nelson Street to see what was happening. I was reminded of this ritual years later when I picked up my friend Keith Meacham in a hired Town Car for a longish ride to Tribeca from the Upper East Side and she emerged from her apartment building with two Scotch-and-waters in sterling-silver julep cups. The driver didn't know what to make of my delight, but then this was Manhattan and he was from Uzbekistan.

A few years ago, a total stranger from Memphis gave me a go cup printed with one of my father's more priceless utterances: "She ain't much in a parlor, but she's hell in a tonk." It's the punch line of a long story that I'd just repeated in a column in the *New York Times,* and even though the guy had no idea who my father was, he had the good sense to appropriate it. This is a safer bet than buying cups with preprinted logos with slogans that tend toward the hackneyed: "Cheers Y'all!" "When in Doubt Wear Camo," "Time flies when you're having RUM!"

Still, there are some good ones. At a dinner party in Montgomery not long ago, my host sent me home with two worth keeping: "S.L.U.T.S" ("Southern Ladies Under Tremendous Stress") and "D.T.M.D.C." (which stands for "Don't Touch

My Damn Cup," helpfully printed with the owner's name). My cousin Linda Jane also turned me on to some good ones from a store in Baton Rouge called Paper N Things where she buys her own considerable cache. Two, involving the same body part, made me laugh out loud: "Does this cup make my ass look BIG?" and "Your boots may be made for walking but mine are in case I need to kick your ASS."

As much as I love—and use—a go cup, I also would like to say a few words in praise of the flask. Not only are flasks elegantly shaped and often very beautiful, they are also crucial to have on hand in times of stress, duress, or just plain boredom. Hemingway, not surprisingly, had a lot—you can see his entire collection at the John F. Kennedy Presidential Library and Museum, where Mary Hemingway sent them from Cuba. Also, there's nothing sexier than a guy who pulls a proper flask from the inside pocket of his blazer or the hip pocket of his chinos, and casually offers you a nip—a guy a lot like Percy himself, who describes doing that very thing in his seminal essay on bourbon.

In the all too common event that such a man is not around, ladies must learn to keep one discreetly tucked into a handbag. I myself learned this lesson the hard way, during the interminable ritual known in my adopted hometown as the Mardi Gras ball. A ball, unlike a parade, is not an occasion where a lady can waltz around carrying a go cup—until recently ladies weren't allowed to drink at all unless a male krewe member deigned to duck "backstage" and mix them a clandestine toddy. Even now, it's not easy. Just prior to the presentation of the debutantes who make up the maids and the queen of the court, the sparsely located bars shut down and everyone is forced to take their seats in uncomfortable hotel ballroom chairs in order to watch an endless stream of girls in white promenade, curtsy, and promenade again for such a long time that you pray to lose consciousness. To the locals, who seem to enjoy themselves immensely, it's like church—it's what they do and they've been doing it so long that the women, at least, manage to do it without alcohol. Not me. So this year, a year in which I will happily attend because I happen to love one of the debs, I have planned ahead. As I type, I have on my desk beside me a very handsome, gracefully curved, six-ounce flask made of English pewter and inscribed with my initials. It was given to me years ago by my very generous friend Anne Buford, along with a case of very old Macallan Scotch. I drank the Scotch, on the rocks, in a nice heavy glass and forgot about the flask. Until now. It is the perfect size for an evening clutch.

Rocking the Boat

THE QUESTION IS THIS: IS A STEREOTYPE BAD IF THE traits it advances are good? I've been polling some of my more enlightened friends, and we've been forced to conclude that the answer is still yes. If, for example, you are of Chinese descent and, therefore, generally assumed to be pretty damn smart, wouldn't you prefer that people think of you as intelligent because you, yourself, as an individual, are, in fact, intelligent? I mean, if you're smart simply by default—by dint of the fact that you happen to be Chinese—you personally don't get all that much credit.

It's not a problem I run into. White Southerners don't get the smart thing too much, even if we also happen to write for a living. My good friend and colleague Roy Blount, Jr., says folks are forever telling him stuff like, "Well, of course you're a writer, you're from the South, you people are natural storytellers." It irritates him. I know how he feels. When the cocktail hour rolls around, my hosts invariably assume that my DNA requires a big slug of bourbon. I drink Scotch. So as generalities go, I have to say that I think I'd prefer being automatically characterized as a natural-born sharp-as-a-tack type rather than a yarn-spinning, corn-pone-munching bourbon swiller who, while we're at it, cannot dance. (And who might just also be the sort of person traditionally and regionally inclined to stereotype people of other races and ethnicities.)

The question arose in August 2015 when the first ever Dragon Boat Festival was held in my hometown of Greenville, Mississippi. In China, the festival is an actual national holiday. But it has since been co-opted by cities across America, especially by those like Greenville that are located on a body of water on which dragon boat teams can race. John Cox III, our stalwart former mayor, had been pushing for the festival ever since taking office two years earlier, as a way to honor the contributions Chinese Americans have made to our local culture. This makes more sense than it might seem. Mississippi has long been home to more Chinese Americans than any other state in the South, and when I was growing up, more than 90 percent of them were in the Mississippi Delta.

The first immigrants turned up around 1870 directly from Sze Yap, in southern China, as recruits of white planters, who were hedging their bets with replacement labor, lest the newly freed slave population take their emancipation a little too seriously. Others made their way east from California while building the transcontinental railroad, and they stuck around to help build the levees. Either way, upon arrival they were not much interested in field labor—or in the rudimentary shacks built to house them. In what might be described as an early sharp-witted move, they turned instead to the grocery store trade, establishing themselves in African-American neighborhoods, catering to a population who had until recently been "paid" in goods like flour or cornmeal from the plantation commissary and who now had (a little) cash to buy their own groceries.

During my childhood, there were still well over a dozen Chinese stores in town—including Min Sang, Toi Roi, Bing's, Ting's, and Joe Gow Nue Nos. 1 and 2—as well as an enormous and enormously popular Chinese restaurant called How Joy. These days, a lot of the population has left the Delta for other parts of the state or beyond (two of my classmates, for example, went off to Stanford and MIT), but lots of folks came back for the festival, which included a delicious six-course banquet the night before the race.

Anyway, I was all for honoring the Chinese and supporting the mayor, and I happened to be home when Howard Brent, the father of my lifelong friend Jessica and one of my personal heroes, said he would sponsor a team if we would get one together. So we gathered a group, named ourselves the Drag Queens, and assembled racing uniforms consisting of hot pink wigs, dangling earrings, and various other accessories including sequined berets and flower-bedecked headbands for the men and women alike. Our theme also enabled me to put to use the leopard-print bra headpiece I made myself when I rode in the Mardi Gras Muses parade, a topper that would be the envy of any real live drag queen—and one so fetching that none other than my former *Vogue* colleague André Leon Talley suggested I wear it to a luncheon at Manhattan's La Grenouille.

We were pumped. It's hard not to be when Howard is your benefactor. He is a man who gets excited by pretty much everything. Growing up, I spent the night in the Brent house more times than I can count, but Jessica and her siblings and I rarely got a full night's sleep. Howard was forever yanking us out of bed: "Y'all get up, let's play the guit-tar"; "Y'all get up, there's a rodeo in Monroe." His enthusiasm is invariably infectious, and his family has been in the towboat business for generations, so he was a natural to go on the local radio to promote the fest.

After some amusing and semi-sexist innuendo about the importance of getting your strokes in sync and your rhythm right (which, I found out, happens to be true), Howard got around to talking about his classmates at Greenville High: "I graduated with Paul Chu Lin and Shirley Wong. I used to try and sit by them, see, because the Chinese were real smart, but they wouldn't let me copy off their papers. So I had to go and find another dumb son of a gun like me to copy off of." He went on to say that sponsorships benefited the Chinese American Cultural Alliance (CACA) scholarship fund and other worthy causes, and that "folks need to write some checks, because we need some more boats out there. They're beautiful. Got a dragon on the front."

Now, you could not find anyone more well intentioned than Howard if you looked hard. Plus, he was really mostly talking about two classmates whose individual smarts he had seen for himself. Also, now that I've been a dragon boat competitor myself, I can back up this particular stereotype with some actual statistics. For example, the number of Chinese-American teams came to exactly one, and it was sponsored by CACA, which sorta had to do it.

The day I turned up for practice at the appointed hour of 11:00 A.M., it was about ninety-eight degrees with no shade in sight. My teammates demonstrated their own good sense by being almost entirely absent. There were five of us, plus two employees of Harlow's casino hotel who had missed their own practice (and who, after all, were being paid to be part of their company's team) and an unsuspecting acquaintance we pressed into duty after he made the mistake of walking his dog within our line of sight. I had on my usual uniform of black pants, black shirt, and black ballet flats because I'd erroneously figured "practice" would consist of eyeballing the boat (a terrifyingly narrow vessel) and maybe testing my grip on the oar. Instead, a very stern woman with a crew cut (who was among the coaches who fly around the country to supervise these races) got us out on the water and forced us to paddle away—very badly and not remotely in sync—for a full hour. Back on shore, one of our group dropped to his knees on the cobblestoned embankment; another threw up. This did not bode well, but on the day of the race, we managed to come in at a respectable fourteenth out of twenty in the first trial and thirteenth in the second.

A team of typically competitive cardiologists came in first, but they didn't seem to have nearly as much fun as we did. Our viewing tent featured a bar complete with Southsides (in keeping with the regatta spirit of things), plus platters of tasty snacks like pimento cheese sandwiches, the enjoyment of which was aided by the fact that we didn't have to stay in fighting (and relatively sober) shape for the finals. In retrospect, I'm a tiny bit bitter that we didn't win for best team spirit, because we certainly had it, but we are not giving up. Our next theme will be Polynesian so we can keep the wigs and add grass skirts—and mai tais, of course.

On my way back to New Orleans, I drove past the small metropolis of Louise, Mississippi, where Hoover Lee still owns and operates his store, Lee Hong. Hoover was mayor of Louise for eighteen years, during which time he visited Reagan in the White House, and he was an alderman for six years before that. His sons Stan and Tim pretty much run the operation now, but Hoover and his wife still live in the house he built in the back, and he still makes his superlative (and secret) Hoover Sauce, which is excellent on wild game and a key ingredient in my friend Hank Burdine's tasty duck poppers.

Anyway, when I stopped in to replenish my sauce stock, I reflected on the fact that when I was a kid, Hoover's store, like most of the rest of the Delta Chinese groceries, still sold live chickens in cages. Which leads me to one of my father's favorite stories, about a stunt pilot named Gaston Hunter (pronounced "Gastone"). Well into the 1960s, the Delta played host to frequent weekend air shows. Apparently Gaston had seen a rather more accomplished pilot whose act consisted of throwing a trained hawk out the open window of his plane. The hawk would glide through the air beautifully, executing a few loop de loops, and when the pilot landed, the hawk would come light on his wrist. Gaston did not have a trained hawk; instead he stopped at what was then called (really, really politically incorrectly) "the Chinaman's store" and bought himself a rooster, which are not renowned for their flying abilities in the first place and which at any rate had clipped wings. As he was executing his last big move, he threw out the rooster, which, naturally, went into a long, sickening spiral, one that makes me cringe to think about, even now, and it hit the ground with a big splat. Gaston was so embarrassed he didn't land and flew all the way to Memphis instead. As for the rooster (and to continue along this increasingly incorrect vein), he did not stand a Chinaman's chance.

And here's where we might possibly have evidence of another stereotype that could just be more or less accurate. There's a reason, after all, that everybody laughs at those "Hey y'all, watch this" jokes. Because we know that in the hands of some of our, um, more redneck brethren, the equivalent of a rooster is going to land at our feet.

Belle of the Ball

I HAVE LOVED DONALD LINK AND STEPHEN STRYJEWSKI, the New Orleans überchefs whose empire includes Herbsaint, Cochon, and Cochon Butcher, for a very long time for lots of good reasons. They fill my plate with delicious food and my glass (all too often) with fine wine. They're smart, they're generous, and they never fail to make me laugh. If all that weren't enough, in January 2015 they enabled me to fulfill a decades-long dream: to attend a masked ball dressed almost entirely in feathers.

The occasion was the first annual Bal Masque, held at the brilliantly renovated Orpheum theater to benefit the Link Stryjewski Foundation, formed to help at-risk kids in our city (of which there are far, far too many). Some of my favorite chefs (including Mike Lata, Frank Stitt, Suzanne Goin, and Nancy Oakes) came from all over the country to cook. John Alexander and William Dunlap made gorgeous paintings that were auctioned off for the cause, and Jimmy Buffett provided typically swell music. I went as a Grand Palm cockatoo, complete with tall crest and orange face. It was a perfect night.

I love a ball, especially one involving masks and costumes, which is ironic really, since I am fairly hopeless on the dance floor. It's not my fault. Girls generally learn to dance by box stepping in time with their fathers, but mine was more of a solo act—he dances as he does pretty much everything, primarily to entertain himself. My mother, who is a phenomenally good dancer, grew up in Nashville, attending Fortnightly Club dances. My generation's versions of Fortnightly were excruciating events at which girls draped their arms around the necks of acne-faced boys and shuffled around in a tight circle to the strains of "Colour My World." As a result, I'm more of a postmidnight kitchen dancer, jumping around solo to, say, Del Amitri on the antiquated boom box. I dance like no one is watching because no one ever *is* watching.

Back to balls: My first experience with the form was at the annual coming-out party put on by the Delta Debutante Club in my hometown of Greenville, Mississippi, where I served as a page at the age of thirteen. The decor that year featured birdcages containing hot-pink parakeets hanging from the ceiling of the country club ballroom. My father and I posed beneath one of the beribboned cages for the photographer Arthur David Greenberg, who had come all the way down from New York for the occasion. Despite the fact that I was dressed in a hideously unflattering white dress complete with a lace bertha collar, it was fun. In the photo, we are trying hard not to crack up at the absurdity of it all, and I cadged lots of contraband champagne. But when it came time to make my actual debut, I politely declined on the grounds that it would've been redundant. I'd already come out to at least one version of society (the one my father invariably referred to as "riffraff") while drinking a series of flaming drinks atop the bar at the late and much lamented One Block East. Also, a few years before what would have been my year, the ball's emcee, a local doctor who was a sweet, sweet man but clearly a little carried away, announced that the debs had "achieved social attainment in the eyes of the Lord." I was not at all convinced that the Lord approved of my shenanigans during that particular period of my life, and I felt it wouldn't have been in the best of taste to pretend.

I could tell my mother was secretly relieved, but my father, awash in misplaced sentiment, called me up in my Georgetown dorm room and asked me if I was sure of my decision: "We could get our picture taken underneath those birds." But then he has always been amused by the decor of the deb ball, which is always held just after Christmas. One year, in the sixties, the ceiling was hung with Spanish moss and the girls' hairdos were especially high. Santa had just brought me a Troll Village, and when Daddy walked into the ballroom, he announced that he felt as though he were inside of one.

There was also the unfortunate year of the Debutanks, in which most of those being presented were a tad on the chubby side. To be fair, it's hard to look svelte when draped in yards of taffeta or tulle or both. When I was a writer at *Vogue*, Jenna and Barbara Bush graciously agreed to pose for us on the occasion of their father's second run for the presidency. It was a coup—they'd never before agreed to do any press—but a fashion editor with an obvious agenda chose to dress them in poufy white Vera Wang gowns. I have never loved Laura Bush more in my life than when she took one look at her daughters and politely remarked that they looked exactly like cupcakes. She was right, of course, and the rack of bouffant frocks was immediately sent packing. Unlike a lot of girls from their home state, neither twin had opted to make her debut, and who can blame them? Such an outing requires the famously extravagant (and body-contorting) Texas Dip, a maneuver that involves nearly touching one's forehead to the floor with gloved arms akimbo, as one's ball dress rises like a giant marshmallow (or, indeed, an elaborately frosted cupcake) from behind.

The lesson here is what I already knew, that it's a whole lot more fun to make like an exotic bird than a cupcake. I achieved my avian look on my own—what I lack in dance floor moves, I more than make up for in glue-gunning skills. (People are always surprised that I'm crafty, which I find a tiny bit offensive.) Before the recent Bal Masque, for example, I purchased $450 worth of feathers online and set up a veritable cottage industry on my living room floor creating looks for my fellow attendees. For inspiration, I turned to the three great balls of the twentieth century at which the guests paid elaborate attention to their masks and headgear. (At one, Salvador Dalí designed Christian Dior's costume and Dior designed Dalí's.) The first, thrown in 1951 by the Mexican silver heir Carlos (Charlie) de Beistegui at his Labia Palace in Venice, featured a troupe of giants, two jazz bands, and a thousand guests, all of whom arrived by gondola, cheered on by hundreds of onlookers lined up along the Grand Canal. Described as the first "mass media" event, it was photographed by Cecil Beaton. In one of the shots, commissioned by *Vogue*, Orson Welles sports an enormous feathered crown not unlike my own Bal Masque crest.

The second "ball of the century" was the Bal Oriental thrown by Baron Alexis de Redé in 1969 at his Paris residence, the exceedingly grand Hôtel Lambert. Here, the giants were replaced by dozens of torch-bearing "Nubians," bodybuilders procured from assorted local gymnasiums and painted black. Clearly, this was long before the era of political correctness, or animal rights awareness either, since one guest arrived toting a baby panther. At least the elephants that greeted the four hundred guests weren't real. Instead, they were constructed of papier-mâché and straddled by live riders beneath ornate gilded canopies. In his memoirs, the baron rather drily describes a guest who came as a pagoda: "She had to be brought to the ball in the back of a truck, as her costume was made out of metal. She could not sit down in the truck and she could not sit down at all until she took it off. You have to make a balance between enjoying the evening, or the impression you want to make. I am not sure she got it right."

Far less restrictive getups were worn to Truman Capote's Black and White Ball, thrown in 1966 at Manhattan's Plaza Hotel in honor of Katharine Graham. Newlyweds Frank Sinatra and Mia Farrow turned up masked as cats; Candice Bergen wore white bunny ears constructed by the young Halston. As at the other two soirées, the guests looked seriously fabulous, but it doesn't sound like they had all that much fun. Bergen later reported that she was so bored at Capote's affair that she left early. Sinatra and his entourage decamped for his favorite dive bar, Jilly's. None of de Beistegui's guests professed to even like him much.

This is a shame because one of the many pluses of a masked ball is that if you are in disguise, you can get up to all sorts of no good with impunity. At the first ball I ever hosted, one of the guests pointed to his camouflage bow tie and cummerbund and announced that he was in hiding from his wife. He was making a joke, and a corny one at that, but I got it. A ball is for dancing with multiple partners, flirting with strangers, trying on one disguise after another even if you don't happen to be in costume. The ball in question, cohosted by my dear friend Jessica Brent, was not, as it happens, a masked occasion. I had recently canceled a wedding and was feeling exuberantly un-masked. (Not long after the cancellation, a friend gave me a birdcage with the door ajar—in retrospect I should have hung those from the ceiling.) Still, like the aforementioned party givers, we had a fantastical theme—just one slightly more in sync with our Mississippi Delta locale.

Instead of life-size elephants, a taxidermy deer welcomed our guests at the front door of the (sadly now burned-down) antebellum house Mount Holly. Inside, wild geese flew above the dance floor, beavers gnawed on logs, and a gigantic logger-head turtle held a bouquet of wildflowers in its mouth. No one brought a live panther, but a stuffed one crouched on a mantel. Music was provided by Terrance Simien & the Mallet Play-boys, a terrific zydeco band from Louisiana that at the time featured a washboard-playing midget who did backflips across the stage. (Let the record show that we were not being remotely politically incorrect—he was an honest-to-God member of the band, not a prop.) Most of the people who would have been at my wedding (except, naturally, for the groom) turned up, and it was exactly as we'd hoped. People danced like crazy and necked on the staircase. My father, true to form, borrowed the wash-board and took to the stage.

Jessica and I called it the Last Annual Hoodoo Mamas Ball and Gumbo a Go Go (don't ask us why), and we've about decided we're due for another, perhaps the Next to Last Annual. In the meantime, I'm already planning my costume for the next Bal Masque. I'm thinking along the lines of some sort of mythical triple-hybrid creature that will allow me to use both horns and feathers. My glue gun is ready.

The Ultimate Party Stop

IT ALL STARTED WHEN MY BUDDY THE WRITER HARTFORD Gongaware turned up in my hometown of Greenville, Mississippi, with some filmmakers who were documenting life in towns along the river. Greenville is a river town (well, sort of—a while ago the river changed course and now we're technically on an oxbow lake called Lake Ferguson, but if you get in a boat at the foot of Main Street, the Mississippi's only about six miles away). Anyway, the camera people needed some footage on the water, and my friends Hank Burdine and Howard Brent offered up their boats for an outing. Because it was the day after the first annual Delta Hot Tamale Festival, there were a lot of people in town, including Roy Blount, Jr., and his wife, the painter Joan Griswold. Naturally, we all decided to go along.

Now, that in itself is not unusual. Pretty much everyone I know in Greenville grew up on a raft or a speedboat or both—we even have a Yacht Club, though to my knowledge only one yacht has actually docked there in its seventy-some-year history. Hank is a commissioner of the Mississippi Levee Board (founded in 1865), and Howard once ran one of the biggest towboat companies in the country (founded by his father, Jesse, a former deckhand, in 1956). We've all spent countless hours water-skiing, tubing, drinking, fishing, and generally engaging in the maritime version of that eternal high school preoccupation "riding around." But this time, we had a destination. We loaded up the boats with buckets of chicken and lots of beer and Bloody Marys and headed straight for an enormous sandbar Hank had found just under the new Jesse Brent Memorial Bridge that connects Mississippi to Arkansas.

Everyone agreed it was magical. On our own private island, we had the freedom of Huck and Jim without the bad guys—if you don't count the evil Asian carp that jumped in the boat and slimed one of the cameras. We ate and drank, and Joan made really cool sculptures out of driftwood. We took dips in the river and lay in the sand and headed back just before sunset beneath a buttermilk sky.

It was already pretty perfect, but since then, our outings have gotten a tad more grandiose. In our second year, we were joined by Bo Weevil, aka Sid Law, who has a welded aluminum boat custom made with a flat bottom, high gunwales, and an eight-foot beam on which he has run the entire length of the Mississippi, Missouri, Tennessee, Arkansas, and Atchafalaya rivers. "Like mine," says Hank, not entirely tongue in cheek, "it was designed exclusively to run safe in the river carrying lots of people, whiskey, and fried chicken."

Bo's boat enabled us to tote more people, but also tables and lounge chairs and a slightly more elaborate menu. There was a full bar and a bartender and a ladies' room in the form of a tepee made from willows cut on the opposite bank. Tunes were provided by the official Sandbar Boombox, a masterpiece of Burdine engineering consisting of an ice chest with holes cut in one side for speakers and a car CD player installed on the inside and rigged with twenty feet of wire attached to a 12-volt battery with alligator clips. There was live music too, provided by the exceptionally talented Brent sisters, Jessica, Eden, and Bronwynne, who all brought their guitars, and Howard, who never goes anywhere without his famous miniature harmonica.

These days, we don't bother to wait for the tamale fest to make a trip, but we do have to wait for the river to go down. (After Hank and I scouted a sandbar for a planned trip in the spring, the river rose six feet in a single day, which meant that it disappeared.) Also, we keep adding stuff: Indian quilts, folding love seats, threadbare Oriental rugs. Hank tops a charcoal-filled hole with a grill in order to cook his sublime duck poppers, and I use it to heat up a big enamel casserole of barbecued pork shoulder. Paper plates and Solo cups have given way to enamel plates and stemmed Lucite glasses. We even have a signature drink, a punch called the Evening Storm (an event we've so far avoided) invented by Christiaan Rollich, the talented bar manager at Suzanne Goin's Lucques and A.O.C. in Los Angeles, after I told him about our exploits and sent him an image of the painting of the same name by David Bates. (At A.O.C., the hostess's mother is from Wilmot, Arkansas, just on the other side of the aforementioned bridge—the world is small, though you could never tell it from our sandbar vantage point.)

On our most recent visit, the river was so low there was

plenty of room for dancing. Eden Brent, the piano virtuoso and three-time Blues Music Award winner, played "Fried Chicken" and "Panther Burn" in her usual performance garb, including a black sequined porkpie hat purchased in the Memphis airport, and lamented the lack of a sandbar keyboard. Our friend Raymond Longoria, who had performed at the tamale fest the day before, had brought his guitar, but not his accordion, at which he excels, so he vowed to return with it next go-round. There were no spoons, so Jessica showed off her prowess with a pair of forks (who knew?). At one point, we hatched a slightly sodden plan to bring out an old upright piano and leave it until the river carried it away the following summer. The next day I got a text from Hank: "Not possible to get an upright on the sandbar. WAY too heavy to transport, but we can do an electric keyboard with a small quiet Honda generator and long cord."

If all this sounds insanely over the top, we come by it naturally. The Mississippi Delta, which is actually the diamond-shaped alluvial floodplain of the Mississippi and Yazoo rivers, was all but uninhabitable until well into the nineteenth century. Lured by some of the richest soil in the world, planters whose land had already been tapped out in places like South Carolina and Kentucky took a gamble and battled panthers and floods and a tangled mess of a hardwood forest before they could even think about dropping a seed into the ground. Once they did, the results were worth it economically, but there wasn't a whole lot to do there, so they became extremely adept at making their own fun. Most of which involved a serious intake of whiskey and traveling long distances over rough terrain—in 1850, fewer than 25,000 people inhabited the Delta's 7,000 or so square miles, and this being the bad old days, the majority of them were slaves. House parties abounded.

These days the population of the Delta is more than 500,000, and there is all manner of things to do, but old habits die hard and we persist in organizing elaborate diversions. I mean, there may be plenty of people, but the mosquitoes and snakes haven't gone anywhere, and it remains hot as hell. Still, there are only so many ways to skin a cat, which is why I can't believe it took us so long to come up with the sandbar as a venue.

Especially since I am apparently no stranger to sandbars, something I was reminded of in a post on my Facebook page a year or so ago by a former bartender at the late and very much lamented One Block East. During what we shall call my formative years, the Block (so called because it was located one block east of the levee) was the primary source of almost every diversion a girl could find. I myself had not planned on sharing any of them—ever—but one day a former assistant checked my page and began reading aloud: "Hey Julia, it's Sam here. Remember that time we stole the DDT's boat and you and Robbie left Finn and me on a sandbar until like five in the morning?" Well, sort of. Sam was a bartender at the Block whom I hadn't heard from in more than thirty years, and the DDT is the *Delta Democrat-Times*, whose then owner, Hodding Carter III, kept a very handsome speedboat docked within walking distance of the bar. Finn is Hodding's daughter, and she knew where the keys were hidden, and Robbie was another bartender with whom I was ridiculously in love. Suffice to say that this is why Facebook scares the hell out of me. Also, my memories are not nearly as clear as Sam's. For example, I have no idea where Robbie and I went while leaving our companions stranded, but I can only hope we found another sandbar and smooched.

It is a miracle that I lived to see another sandbar in the day-light, but I'm extremely grateful that I did. On that last outing, we'd just started unloading the boats and setting up the food tables when a thirteen-foot canoe, outfitted with a tattered American flag and containing two very sun-brown young folks, came within our line of sight. We are used to seeing the occa-sional towboat, and in the old days we'd get a lot of hippies on handmade rafts, most of whom ended up composing the kitchen staff at the Block. But I'm not sure I'd ever seen such a comparatively tiny vessel, especially one that started off in Indiana.

The intrepid canoers, Susan and George, were on their way to Baton Rouge, where they planned to sell the boat and head back north. When we met them, they'd been on the river for more than two months, camping out on sandbars and making infrequent trips into towns for supplies. When they came upon our own elaborate "campsite"—not to mention Hank waving his arms, hollering "Cold beer! Cold beer!"—they must have thought it was a mirage.

They stopped anyway and turned out to be the loveliest of guests. Among Susan's possessions was a beautiful six-string guitar stored in a black plastic garbage bag, and she played a song she'd been composing on the trip. We fed them catfish pâté and barbecue, and then Bo Weevil insisted that he put them up for a few days, promising to drive them and the canoe down to Vicksburg so they could make up for lost time. We showed them around the Delta and invited them to a dove-hunt break-fast and shared all the other diversions we had mastered. They later wrote really nice things about us on their own Facebook page (one on which I came out a lot better), but they did more for us than we did for them. Our encounter reminded us again of the river's mythical but no less real place in American life. It allows for reinvention and renewal, and enables—encourages, really—our citizenry to light out for parts unknown. In our case, new territory is just a twenty-minute boat ride away, but it feels like another world entirely and it makes for a damn fine day.

Songs of the South

A FEW YEARS AGO, I ATTENDED A SIXTIETH BIRTHDAY bash at the House of Blues in New Orleans, and since the birthday boy happened to be a billionaire, the entertainment was especially stellar. My buddy Harry Shearer, a very funny man (and the voice of about half the cast of *The Simpsons*), emceed the proceedings, which kicked off with a version of "Happy Birthday" by his wife, the Welsh chanteuse Judith Owen, that made Marilyn Monroe's seem wholesome. Dr. John cut loose with "Right Place Wrong Time," and Chrissie Hynde, looking and sounding at least as hot as she did when she first broke through with the Pretenders, did a set that included "Don't Get Me Wrong" and "Back on the Chain Gang." The late Gregg Allman was up next with "Statesboro Blues," "One Way Out," and "Melissa," and the great Joe Walsh (who sang an especially ironic "Life's Been Good") closed the show with a rousing set that rocked the house. Or at least it should have.

Before I go any further, I should confess that I have never actually met my host. I was a guest of a guest, and a very lucky one at that, so I am trying to be very careful not to cast aspersions. But it was . . . weird. No one seemed to take much joy in the proceedings, or if they did it was seriously internalized. Though the party was held in what is essentially a big bar, the audience seemed airlifted in from Carnegie Hall. I mean, I learned to make out with the Allman Brothers on the stereo; there's no way to listen to "Melissa" without the hair on the back of your neck standing up. I first heard Joe Walsh when I was ten and he was in the James Gang. Until he joined the Eagles, no one in that band could have pulled off that central guitar riff in "Life in the Fast Lane," which he also played that night. There was some serious history—and not just my own—on that stage.

In contrast to the rest of the group, my friend and I spent the evening juking around like maniacs—or, indeed, like normal people listening to a kick-ass lineup of some of the greatest and most storied musicians in the world. And we weren't just the only ones moving, we were the only ones on our feet—except, of course, the musicians, most of whom were the oldest people in the room. At the time, Gregg Allman was sixty-five and was the recipient of a new liver; Dr. John and Joe Walsh have put enough bad stuff in their bodies over the years to kill a herd of water buffalo. But all three of them exhibited far more energy than the people they were playing for. But then, almost nobody in the audience, which included Bill Gates, was from the South. Apparently, folks in other regions do not spend the bulk of their youths in cars and bars learning about life and love and lust to the beat of a constant sound track.

Which leads me to the definition of Southern music. You

could make the case that most music is Southern since the South gave the world jazz, blues, rock and roll, country, and the songs of Johnny Mercer. But I think you can also define music as Southern by the way you listen to it. In the car, of course, with the AC blasting and the windows rolled down, while banging out the beat on the steering wheel. Or in a club, while dancing the shag or the funky chicken or the gator or trying to do James Brown's splits. It was the Godfather who said, "The one thing that can solve most of our problems is dancing." My friend Humphreys McGee does an indescribable dance during the instrumental break in Rufus Thomas's "Walking the Dog" that is such an intense expression of the good stuff in Humphreys's soul he only does it every five years or so, lest he have a heart attack. When André Leon Talley saw Humphreys "walk the dog" at my parents' house once, he pronounced it a "piece of Appalachian folk art" and said he ought to be in the Smithsonian. Humphreys himself says simply that the song allows "an opportunity to abandon all inhibitions and release my body to my id."

The world would definitely be a better (or at least a more exciting) place if we all tried that every once in a while, but for starters you'd have to get up out of your seat. When I was eleven, I came home from school to find my mother dancing through the house while "American Pie" blared from our brand-new quadraphonic speakers. She was so into it and so oblivious of my presence that I was in awe and maybe even a tiny bit afraid, and I didn't tell her I'd seen her until years afterward. My mother is a great, great dancer. I am not, but that has not kept me from dancing on bars and tables and in my kitchen by myself late at night. Mostly, though, I listen to a lot of music, and below I've created an entirely arbitrary Southern Playlist. If it were remotely comprehensive it would include additional acts ranging from Irma Thomas to the Avett Brothers, but I'll get to them. Fortunately, I have a little bit of time before I start planning my own sixtieth birthday concert (which will likely be broadcast via iPod).

"I'll Take You There"

THE STAPLE SINGERS

Former Stax Records executive Al Bell wrote this song in his daddy's backyard after attending the funeral of his little brother. Much of its power comes from the Memphis Horns and the famed Muscle Shoals Rhythm Section (pay special attention to that bass line), but Mavis Staples's vivid contralto provides plenty of competition. The song may have been written as a classic call-and-response gospel chorus, but she sings it like she is well on her way to a very different kind of heaven.

"Baby, Please Don't Go"/"Gloria"

VAN MORRISON

Morrison is from Northern Ireland, but then so are a whole lot of people in the South. A cover of the Big Joe Williams classic "Baby, Please Don't Go" was the A side of a single recorded by Morrison's band Them in 1964, while "Gloria," written by Van himself, was the B side. In his book *Rock and Roll: The 100 Best Singles,* Paul Williams writes that "here is something so good, so pure, that if no other hint of it but this record existed, there would still be such a thing as rock and roll." The night I met my ex-husband, who was in his former life the lead singer of a band called the Mersey Shores, he played "Gloria" on the piano, and it may well be the reason I married him. The song remains a perfect, raunchy, three-chord rock anthem and such a garage band staple that Dave Barry once joked that "you can throw a guitar off a cliff, and as it bounces off rocks on the way down, it will, all by itself, play 'Gloria.'"

"Turn on Your Love Light"

BOBBY "BLUE" BLAND

This is the kind of song that can—and will—change your life. Much of the intensity comes from the drums of John "Jabo" Starks, who went on to play for James Brown, but, man, it's all there. "The chord changes, the solid horn section, the drum break—none of it has ever been equaled and certainly not surpassed," says my good friend the artist Bill Dunlap, who was himself a drummer. "And then there's Bobby's plaintive call to 'turn on the love light' and 'let it shine on me,' which pretty much sums up the American dream—and which, in the South, always tended to be wetter than in other parts of the world." Enough said.

"The Weight"

THE BAND

Robbie Robertson wrote this masterpiece—chock-full of biblical allusions and characters from bandmate Levon Helm's

Arkansas upbringing—after his first trips south to Memphis from his native Canada. "It was like, 'Whoa, this is where this music grows in the ground, and [flows from] the Mississippi River'," Robertson told a reporter after Helm's death last year. The gospel arrangement of "The Weight," performed with the Staple Singers and featured in Martin Scorsese's *The Last Waltz*, is guaranteed to make you cry.

"Ode to Billie Joe"

BOBBIE GENTRY

Forget all the mystery surrounding the events on the Tallahatchie Bridge; what "Ode to Billie Joe" really captures better than any novel is what happens around a Southern dinner table. And then of course, there's Gentry's deep/smoky/sultry/haunting voice.

"What'd I Say"

RAY CHARLES

I'm pretty sure Ray Charles never wrote a bad song, but if I had to pick just one to listen to for the rest of my life, this would be it. "What'd I Say" was born in 1959 at a dance in Pittsburgh where Charles and the band ran out of songs just before the end of a set that was contracted for four hours. "So I began noodling—just a little riff that floated into my head," Charles explained years later. "One thing led to another and I found myself singing and wanting the girls to repeat after me. . . . Then I could feel the whole room bouncing and shaking and carrying on something fierce." It remained his closing number for the rest of his career.

"I've Got News for You"

EDGAR WINTER

Ray Charles wrote this song too, but I have to say I prefer this version. Edgar and his brother, Johnny, both albino guitar players with roots in Leland, Mississippi, are literally the whitest blues singers alive.

"Polk Salad Annie"

TONY JOE WHITE

In addition to the Swamp Fox's sexy, gravelly voice, this song features the immortal phrase "'Cause her mama was working on a chain gang," as well as White's "chomp, chomp" after the line about the gators getting Granny. Another classic recorded in Muscle Shoals, Alabama.

"Here Comes My Girl"

TOM PETTY AND THE HEARTBREAKERS

Petty, organist Benmont Tench, and guitarist Mike Campbell created a stone classic of a song. Heartbreaking in the best kind of way, it sounds like summer and sex and the first time you've ever heard that title line. Worth it alone for Petty's "Watch her walk."

"Sweet Home Alabama"

LYNYRD SKYNYRD

Three words: "Turn it up."